CHILDREN
in the
MIDDLE AGES

THE LAURA SHANNON SERIES
IN FRENCH
MEDIEVAL STUDIES

CHILDREN
in the
MIDDLE AGES
Fifth–Fifteenth Centuries

by
DANIÈLE ALEXANDRE-BIDON
DIDIER LETT

Preface by Pierre Riché
Translation by Jody Gladding

THE UNIVERSITY OF NOTRE DAME PRESS
Notre Dame, Indiana

Translated by Jody Gladding from the French *Les enfants au Moyen Âge*,
published by Hachette Littératures, Paris, France, in the series La Vie Quotidienne.

The publisher is grateful to
THE FRENCH MINISTRY OF CULTURE—CENTRE NATIONAL DE LIVRE
for support of the costs of translation.

© Hachette Littératures 1997

Library of Congress Cataloging-in-Publication Data
Alexandre-Bidon, Danièle.
    [Enfants au Moyen Age.   English]
    Children in the Middle Ages : fifth-fifteenth centuries / by
  Danièle Alexandre-Bidon, Didier Lett ; préface de Pierre Riché :
  translation by Jody Gladding.
        p.   cm.
    Includes bibliographical references and index.
    ISBN 0-268-02350-6 (cloth : alk. paper) ISBN 0-268-02352-2 (pbk : alk. paper)
    1. Children—Europe—History.   2. Europe—History—476-1492.
  3. Social history—Medieval, 500-1500.   I. Lett, Didier.
  II. Title.
  HQ792.E8A3813   2000
  305.23'094'0902—dc21   99-37711

∞The paper used in this publication meets the minimum requirements of the American National
Standard for Information Sciences—Permanence of Paper for Printed Library Materials,
ANSI Z39.48-1984.

CONTENTS

PREFACE

Who would have thought, a few years ago, an "Everyday Life" of the children of the Middle Ages could be written? Indeed, the standard line was that in this period, children interested adults so little that documentation regarding them was very scant, and therefore, it was nearly impossible to reconstruct their history. Fortunately, we now know that these ideas were ill-founded, this book being proof of that. The texts which mention children are quite numerous and varied. Recently, the author of a work on childhood in medieval Germany listed nearly two hundred sources for this subject. Of course, we must distinguish indirect sources (novels, encyclopedias, legal texts, lives of the saints, etc.) from first-hand accounts like pedagogical texts of which there are dozens, some of them still unpublished: a tract or letter from an abbot to a novice, from a father or mother to his or her son, from a master to a student, from a cleric to a young aristocrat or son of a prince.

This documentation is further enhanced by visual images and archaeological finds. The exposition, *L'Enfance au Moyen Age* [Childhood in the Middle Ages], organized during the winter of 1994–1995 by the Bibliothèque Nationale de France and visited by more than fifty thousand people, demonstrated how children were represented in many miniatures—and not only the Infant Jesus—and how they asserted their presence through the objects that belonged to them: cradles, toys, dishes, writing tablets, etc.

Relying on all this evidence and drawing from an ever-increasing bibliography, the authors of this book give us a work which is very learned, but at the same time, very lively. We discover children, boys and girls, within their popular as well as their aristocratic milieus, from birth—and even before birth—to adolescence, in the bosom of their families, at school, in the fields, in their apprenticeships. Unfortunately, we also discover the unhappy childhood—an ever-present problem—of young ones who are abused, abandoned, prostituted, left to wander and to beg. The Church takes an interest early on in childhood and education because, as Gerson said at the beginning of the fifteenth century, "childhood is the conduit for Church reform." In the high Middle Ages, monks received oblates in their monasteries, after which time clerics directed schools and choir schools and supervised the religious education of the young.

Of course, since I am speaking of the high Middle Ages, I should point out that documentation is not consistent throughout the medieval millennium. The reader will notice that, given the current state of our research, literary and icono-graphical documentation increases beginning from the twelfth century. It will also be apparent that certain geographical sectors take precedence, France, Italy, England, while the children in Spain, Germany, and among Jewish populations are less present. All this is inevitable because we are, in fact, just beginning our inquiry. It will be necessary to extend it even to Islamic countries and the East. This book can serve as incentive for further research. It would be time and effort well spent.

Pierre Riché

INTRODUCTION

Studying the history of childhood may seem innocuous and without dangers. Nevertheless, for many decades now, historians have been far from agreement on this subject which lends itself to controversy.

In 1960, Philippe Ariès published *L'Enfant et la vie familiale sous l'Ancien Régime* [The Child and Family Life under the Ancient Regime].[1] It is the first attempt to synthesize the history of the child in "traditional societies." The child truly becomes an object of history. Reissued in 1973, the work met with formidable success with the general reader and is still widely read today. Let us briefly summarize the author's thesis: the child does not exist in the mind of men and women in the Middle Ages. An "awareness of childhood" and concern for education are recent phenomena, originating with the eighteenth century. According to Philippe Ariès, in the medieval period, "one could not become too attached to anything which might be a lost cause."[2] "If the child happened to die, one was not terribly disturbed by it."[3]

The radical position adopted by the author triggered passionate interest on the part of readers and among his colleagues. An argument was then mounted, following the works of Pierre Riché,[4] Jean-Louis Flandrin,[5] and Emmanuel Le Roy Ladurie.[6] Taking all these critiques into account, Philippe Ariès qualified his positions in a long preface to the 1973 edition of his work. Seven years later he confessed, "I regret not being better informed on the Middle Ages, of which my book speaks so little."[7] Unfortunately, while the originator of these claims qualified them, his emulators would go even further than their model in refuting any awareness of childhood. Edward Shorter, for example, finds mothers in ancient societies to be totally indifferent to children under two years old and asserts that, in the hands of "lower class" parents, the cradle was a "stupefying device."[8] As for Elisabeth Badinter, who is not a historian and whose book, *L'Amour en plus* [Love, Besides] was itself a notorious success, she does not hesitate to claim that prior to the beginning of the nineteenth century, the West was a "society without love," that maternal affection did not exist, and that the child, spurned "like a plaything or a machine . . . was a source of fear."[9] Perhaps our hidden need to believe that love for children is a recent breakthrough, as a way to ennoble our otherwise tragic current history, is the origin of this misunderstanding that has led to the belief in an absence of love and tenderness with regard to children in ancient times.

Thirty-seven years have passed since the publication of Philippe Ariès' book. Today, most of his ideas have been demolished.[10] But to challenge his theses is to breathe life into the problems he raises. Undeniably, it is these problems which have set the direction for the principle research, the historians attempting, first of all, to show childhood in a positive light and to bring out the affection and educational concerns of parents.[11]

One goal of our present work is, certainly, to synthesize all these contributions to the research, but we also hope to point out that channels of inquiry exist other than those opened by Philippe Ariès. Does this idea of dating "the discovery of childhood" really make any sense? To bring to light evidence of parental love is important, of course, because it allows Ariésian theories, still too widely circulated, to be challenged, but that is a feasible undertaking for all periods of history. Being able to step back now, because of the time which separates us from the original work, we can leave the debate and, not only evoke the children known and cherished within the family, but show, too, that medieval society, just as is the case with ours today, was capable of lapses in a certain number of areas concerning the early years of life.

In the following pages, we hoped to touch upon children in all the many countries of present-day Europe. We also wanted to cover the entire medieval period, that is, the ten centuries separating the end of the Roman Empire from the "Great Discoveries," and, as a result, to show an evolution in the perception of childhood, always bearing in mind that what we know about children is only a product of how adults view them. We have considered all children of all ages—including older children and adolescents—and not just the very young, to which recent historiography has paid special attention for some time. Of course it is important to observe them within the context of "family life," but it is equally important to see them within other contexts: school, the fields, work, etc., just as it is necessary to reinsert them into the contexts of the wars, epidemics, and famines marking the beginning and end of the Middle Ages. It is also important to retain a complex view of the child and to widen our understanding of our subject, to distinguish more clearly between girls and boys, and to show the child within different social strata.

To write a history of childhood is to exploit all the resources at our disposal. We have made extensive use of written documents: chronicles, civil and canonical law codes, penitentials, legal proceedings, lives of the saints, accounts of miracles, novels. All this documentation must be deciphered insofar as the children appearing there are perceived through the distorted lens of the clergy, who were, at least until the thirteenth century, nearly the only ones to leave any written record. But we have integrated recent and conclusive archaeological contributions as well. This science has provided precise demographic information, shed light on funeral rituals, and altered in a positive way the image of medieval children and adult attention paid to them. Numerous toys—small soldiers, miniature horses and boats, tea sets, dolls, rattles, wooden swords—are now being discovered almost throughout Europe. Baby's bottles, furniture, dishes, clothes, and jewelry that belonged to children are unearthed and give us, paradoxically, an image of childhood that is very much alive.

We have also made use of iconography. The argument over the existence of an awareness of childhood was originally grounded on an appeal to the image, which Philippe Ariès—and this is another point to his credit—was one of the first to consider as a historical source in and of itself. But the results he obtained by considering a small sample do not correspond at all to those obtained from a collection, still growing, of many thousands of images. Here again, systematic iconographical study weakens the positions of Philippe Ariès.[12]

To speak of medieval children is to evoke equally their representation by adults and their symbolic place in Christian ideology and their material lives and actual place in society. Also, we thought it necessary to first consider specific aspects of the perception of childhood in the early Middle Ages, a perception which determines and explains the whole history of medieval childhood, and then to show, following a plan both chronological and thematic, how children lived and died between the fifth and eleventh centuries, a period marked by difficult conditions, before approaching the emotional and educational environment of the child within the family during the central Middle Ages. Finally we concerned ourselves with the different children populating the texts and images of the fourteenth and fifteenth centuries, in the fields, in the streets, in apprenticeships, in the castles, and at school. The documentation from the end of the medieval period is much more plentiful than what has been left for us from earlier centuries and allows for much more confident elaboration upon the history of the actual life of children.

THE CHILD
in
CHRISTENDOM

Fifth–Thirteenth Centuries

Didier Lett

ONE

The Christian Family
and Relations

The Gradual Lessening of Paternal Power

In Rome, the father held absolute power over all the members of his family (*patria potestas*). He held the power of life and death over his child. In "raising up" the newborn if it were a boy, or in ordering that she be taken to the breast if it were a girl, the father indicated to his family and society that he accepted responsibility for nurturing his progenitor. If he did not do so, he indicated that he refused it.[1] As long as the son or daughter had not yet left the paternal *domus*, he or she could not escape his legitimate control. However, under the late Empire, the ever more blatant intervention of the state in the private domain and the growing influence of stoicism (self-control and concern for others) led to a relaxation of the father's legal hold over the child. From the beginning of the second century B.C., in the case of abusive punishment, the son in a family was able to appeal against his father to a magistrate who, if the case warranted it, would grant him his freedom. The sale of children was forbidden, and the possibilities for abandoning them limited. The legislation of the first Christian emperors, beginning from Constantine, early in the fourth century, pointed in the same direction: paternal authority could be revoked in cases where, for example, the father exposed the child, offered his daughter for prostitution, or was himself involved in incestuous behavior.

Though limited, this paternal power remained no less important in the high Middle Ages, as certain conciliar decisions indicated. In May 541, the Canon 22 of the Council of Orleans forbade, under pain of excommunication, the marriages of daughters without the parental authorization. The second canon of another council held in the same city a few years earlier (in 511) required anyone who ran away with a woman to return her to her father and become his slave or to pay him a ransom until the consenting woman was able to obtain paternal pardon.

But, despite everything, both in the law and in practice, paternal power was growing weaker. With society becoming Christianized, paternal *pietas* limited *potestas* to a greater and greater extent. But more importantly, if the power of the father slackened, it was because the power of God the Father competed with it, outflanked it, and surpassed it.

A New Relationship

From the very beginning of the Judeo-Christian tradition, there has been a remarkable contradiction with regard to the love between parents and children. The scriptural texts continually maintain that, following the fourth commandment (Exodus 20:12), one must honor and love one's father and mother, but at the same time, spiritual kinship must take precedence over kinships of flesh and blood, even to the point of sacrificing one's son if God demands it, as in the example of Abraham. On many occasions, Christ declares: "Whoever loves his father or mother more than me is not worthy of me. Whoever loves his son or his daughter more than me is not worthy of me" (Matthew 10:37). "If someone comes to me without despising his father, his mother, his wife, his children, his brothers, his sisters, and even his own life, he cannot be my disciple" (Luke 14:26). The Church Fathers and the earliest theologians returned to this idea and provided commentary. For Saint Augustine, for example, Christ teaches us "to let our spiritual relationship come before our flesh and blood relationships."[2] Moreover, with the help of his mother, he himself seems to have applied the precepts he defends. Speaking of his father, he addresses God in this way: "My mother did everything possible so that you were my father, you, my God, more than him."[3]

Thus a completely new and original conception of kinship was created, based upon a hierarchy. Presented as models, the saints always rejected earthly relations, a rejection all the more necessary at the very beginning of Christianity, a period in which most of the parents of future saints were pagans. When the child–saint benefited from parental support in realizing his or her vocation, it is not surprising that it nearly always came from the mother, who had sometimes already adopted the Christian religion. Thus, the rupture from the father symbolized a negation of the old order marked by paternal authority and paganism.

There are numerous examples of young saints who established their distance with regard to their parents, sometimes very early. The future St. Nicholas decided from birth to nurse from his mother only two times a week (Wednesday and Thursday).[4] This precocious young one illustrates the inferiority of maternal nourishment in comparison to heavenly nourishment. As the saint grew up, he always remained outside of familial pleasures, refusing to participate in his brothers' and sisters' games, preferring to go to the church to listen to the services, pray, or memorize his psalter. If he did play with other children his own age, he diverted the game into edifying ends. This is how the hagiographer* Frédéric de Hallum speaks of the young saint:

> The mother of Frédéric possessed a few sheep, for which he became the shepherd, in the manner of David. But while his companions frolicked

---

*Words included in the glossary are marked with an asterisk the first time they appear in the text.

and conducted themselves with the lightheartedness of youth, he never joined in their games; but he applied himself to repeating the Lord's Prayer which his mother had taught him, or he even constructed little churches, or altars made from interweaving the pages of books. In short, he imitated the actions of the clergy in every way and to the extent that he could. . . .[5]

The rejection of the biological family hit with particular virulence at the time of marriage, the sacrament which was the base of life in this century, and one unacceptable for the future saint. According to hagiographic sources, the adolescent nearly always came into conflict with parents when the latter, putting the marriage union before the vocation of their child, tried unsuccessfully to impose matrimony upon him or her. The refusal faced by the parents served as a ecclesiastical model in two ways. First, it showed that realizing one's religious vocation must take precedence over obedience to parents. Second, it served as a reminder that marriage cannot take place without the free consent of the couple in question.

Beginning from the Carolingian period especially, the Church determined the new contours of kinship. It struggled against the common practice of abduction and combatted incest. Readopting the Roman system of computing* kinship, it established a ban on marriage up to the seventh degree of relatedness, and that remained in effect until the Fourth Latran Council (1215) which, in order to better adapt to the reality of the situation, re-established this ban up to the fourth degree according to the Roman system. This legislation was fundamental because, for the Church, marriage constituted the only legitimate framework for procreation. In Roman and Germanic societies, polygamy and cohabitation seem to have been relatively widespread, at least in the upper levels of society, upon which documentation sheds the most light. Even if, beginning from the second or third century, pagan Roman aristocrats participated in the "promotion of marriage" which created a new internal ethics for couples,[6] the notion of the legitimate child remained vague and repudiations by spouses were frequent. The high Middle Ages largely inherited these practices, despite numerous prohibitions by the councils. In his *Historia Francorum*, Gregory of Tours is often obliged to distinguish between the sons of legitimate wives and those of concubines when designating the various children of the Merovingian kings. Moreover, he clearly states, "One now calls king's sons all those whom the kings have engendered."[7] In the Carolingian period, important legislation aimed at promoting monogamy and the indissolubility of marriage (for example, in the famous *Admonitio generalis* of 789).

But, despite the condemnations of the Church, the bastard was still held in relatively high regard. Thierry, the eldest son of Clovis, was born of a concubine, which did not in the least prevent him from receiving an inheritance equal to that of his brothers. The same is true for Sigebert, the natural son of Dagobert. In the high Middle Ages, the natural children of royal and aristocratic families had the same inheritance rights as the legitimate children. Offspring issuing from the seed of the father, from no matter what womb, were integrated into the family and the lineage. The gradual exclusion of bastards must wait for the establishment of Gregorian marriage and a much greater "moralization" of society, beginning at the end of the eleventh century.

The Confirmation of Procreation and Pregnancy

Matrimonial union must result in procreation to take on Christian meaning. In the eyes of the Church, procreation is the sole justification for the sexual act, as Pope Gregory the Great (590–604) reminds us, for example, in his response addressed to the archbishop of Canterbury, Augustine: "a carnal tie is absolutely necessary, but it must be prescribed by procreation, not sensual pleasure."[8] That is how parents respect the words that God addresses to Noah and his sons: "Be fruitful, multiply, fill the earth" (Genesis 9:1).

Many accounts of miracles present infertile couples who, by divine intercession, obtain the long-awaited child or describe perilous deliveries saved by the intervention of a saint or the Virgin. In the high Middle Ages, this theme was sometimes used to show the superiority of the Christian God over pagan deities and to persuade kings to convert. At the beginning of the seventh century, King Edwin of Northumbria celebrated the birth of his daughter, Eanfled, and thanked his gods. But the bishop Paulinus, present at the event, began to glorify the God of the Christians. He told the king that if the queen had delivered a child without too much pain, it was thanks to the prayers that he had addressed to God during parturition. At these words, the king rejoiced and promised to convert if the God of the Christians would grant him life and assure him victory over his enemies. To seal his commitment, he agreed to have his daughter baptized in the Christian religion.[9]

From the beginning of the sixth century, the barbarian law codes also show the extent to which the pregnant woman was protected. The compensatory fines paid to the victim or her family in case of injury or murder (wergeld*) increased largely as a function of the loss suffered by the injured party. Now, the tariff paid for a crime perpetrated against a pregnant woman was always extremely high. In Salic law, for example, the one who killed a free young woman of childbearing age had to pay 600 sous, and 700 if she was pregnant, which represented the maximum fee. On the other hand, the one who killed a woman past menopause only had to pay 200 sous. In Visigothic law, the individual who killed a woman of childbearing age was punished by a fine of 250 sous, nearly as much as for the murder of a free adult male (300 sous), who, of age to bear arms, represented inestimable worth in this warlike society. Reading Visigothic law, it is astonishing how small a case is made for the newborn, since the one who killed a male baby only had to pay 60 sous (30 sous if it was a girl). In fact, even if it was a crime to kill an unweaned infant, since punishable by a fine, the act was judged four times less serious than the murder of a mother who, alive, would be capable of producing many children, of assuring the continuation of life. In the value system of barbaric law, it was first and foremost a matter of reprimanding most severely those who caused injury to economic and familial holdings, and, in a Christianized society (and the barbaric law codes largely took the expansion of this new religion into account), those who have struck a blow against the sacred.

Pregnancy is one of the conditions which redeems the Christian woman, as clearly expressed by Saint Paul: "Nonetheless she will be saved by becoming a mother, if she continues in faith, love, and holiness, with modesty" (1 Timothy 2: 15). Thus, Christianity reconsidered pregnancy and exalted the pregnant woman as it also gave value to the fetus. In antiquity, the voice or gestures of the infant in the mother's womb often announced a misfortune. For Christians, on the contrary, these were happy omens, as with John the Baptist "who leapt for joy" in the womb of his mother Elizabeth, when the pregnant Mary visited (Luke 1:39–45). Many future saints give signs which announce their holiness *in utero*. This re-interpretation of an ancient pre-Christian theme, giving it positive meaning, indicates clearly how, beginning from the scriptures, Christianity put increased value on the period of pregnancy and attributed a personality to the fetus.

The Fear of Infertility

Thus, a prolific family was perceived as a Christian family which was fulfilled, which followed the evangelical precepts. On the contrary, infertility was a mark of sin. The finger was pointed at married couples without children. In the Middle Ages, many foods and drinks were reputed to increase the fertility of the male (leeks, carrots, asparagus) or the female (mandrake root), and there were just as many places of worship—and not always Christian worship—fountains, sacred springs, or rocks upon which a certain number of rituals were performed, sanctuaries specializing in the struggle against infertility.

The years of sterility for a couple were particularly agonizing. "What terrible sin could I have committed to make me unable to procreate?" the man and the woman each ask themselves. But this long wait was also a source of hope, the hope of conceiving an exceptional being offered by God as recompense, "as if a long wait was only the slow ripening of a perfect fruit."[10] Those who could not have children remembered all the sterile couples of the Bible who, by divine grace, finally conceived: Ishmael (Genesis 16), Isaac, awaited for ninety years (Genesis 21), Samuel (1 Samuel 1:4–20), or John the Baptist (Luke 1:7). In imitation of these scriptural figures, many saints were born after a period of infertility for the parents who, in order to obtain divine intervention, sometimes promised that the child would be destined for the spiritual life.

Even if it is now known that a couple's sterility can be attributed as often to the husband as to the wife, in the high Middle Ages, it was nearly always the wife who was held responsible. There are numerous cases of men repudiating their mates for their infertility. Certainly, penitence rituals punished this deplorable practice, but the canonists and theologians proved to be very uncomfortable when it came to justifying a childless marriage. We have no doubt arrived at the crux of a contradiction within the system of Christian beliefs, at the crossroads of two dogmas: the indissolubility of marriage and the necessity of procreation to justify the carnal act.

Abnormal Births

A child born deformed or defective was perceived as the consequence of demonic intervention or divine punishment. We know of the medieval belief in "changelings." It sometimes happened that the devil replaced an infant for a demonic being which could be recognized by its incessant crying and its extreme thinness even when it ate a lot.[11] Here is how they were described by Guillaume d'Auvergne at the beginning of the thirteenth century:

> I cannot avoid mentioning those little children called changelings among the common people, and of whom the old women never stop talking, saying they are the sons of demons, hatched; the latter substitute their own children for the children of women, so that these women will feed them as if they were their own. That is why they are called "changelings" (*cambiones*), that is to say, changed, or exchanged, or substituted for the infants born of the women. It is said that they are thin, that they cry incessantly, and that they are greedy for milk, so greedy that four wet-nurses could not keep just one of them happy. They seem to remain with their nurses for many long years, and then to fly away, or more often, vanish.[12]

The first cries of the nursling are disturbing, troubling, even unbearable. They were often interpreted by the clergy as a sign of a person's sinful condition or as a manifestation of the devil. That is why recipes existed for quieting these cries. The women doctors of the School of Salerno recommended administering poppy. The *Decretum* of Burchard of Worms, from the beginning of the eleventh century, mentions a practice consisting of making the child pass through a tunnel in the earth to stop its cries.[13] This practice attests to the prophylactic power attributed to the earth by an essentially rural society and the extent to which their children's sobs concerned and worried parents.

A child's abnormality could also be perceived as a divine punishment. Gregory of Tours reports the case of a woman from the Berry who gave birth to a monster:

> What a subject of mockery it was to look at for many, and when the mother was asked how she could have given birth to such a child, she confessed in tears that it had been conceived during a Sunday night. And not daring to kill it, as mothers were in the habit of doing, she raised it as if it were normal.[14]

Even if the extreme precision of the conception date seems hardly credible, for the mother, as for the entire family, this monstrous infant was the clear sign of its parents' sinfulness, for which they had to do penitence by raising it . . . just as one carries his own cross. This *exemplum** effectively served the Church's discourse; following this story, Gregory of Tours reminds us that there are enough days in the week for sensual pleasure, and it is necessary to respect the Sabbath rest. He states specifically, "If couples unite in embraces on this day, the sons born of this union will be crippled or epileptic or leprous."

Multiple births were also seen as the sign of sin. If a woman delivered many children, it was because she had had sexual relations with many men. Paul Diacre mentions, for example, the extraordinary story of a prostitute who delivered seven babies on the same day.[15] In about 1170, Marie de France relates the story of a woman who delivers twins. Her neighbor then mocks the husband and calls into question the young mother's fidelity:

> If his wife has had two sons,
> They are both dishonored
> Because we know very well what's happened:
> You have never seen
> And you will never see
> A woman giving birth
> To two infants at one time,
> Unless two men have made them for her

Happily, the honor of the wife is saved in the eyes of God because:

> That same year, the slanderer
> Becomes pregnant
> Pregnant with two babies:
> So her neighbor is avenged![16]

All of these beliefs together convey the anguish and powerlessness of a society faced with the abnormal.

The Christian Meaning of Maternity: Birth, Churching, and Nursing

The necessary redemption of the woman through maternity, beginning with her pregnancy, is followed by labor pains and delivery, a *postpartum* quarantine, and her reintegration into the Church through the ceremony of churching.

All sources seem to be in agreement here, leaving us with the image of difficult, painful, and sometimes fatal deliveries. "There is no greater pain than toothache and labor," affirms the medieval proverb. Women about to give birth are often in pain for many days before delivery; when they do not die, they sometimes suffer serious after-effects: blindness, tumors, or paralysis. Without a doubt, these perilous deliveries were a reality. However, in the accounts directed toward edifying ends, to give such a picture of suffering proceeded also from didactic intent. These scenes obliged the Christian to call to mind again some words from the scriptures. As Gregory the Great reminds us,

> there is sensual pleasure in procreation, pain in childbirth. That is why it is said to the first mother of all men, "You will give birth in pain."[17]

In the twelfth century, the hagiographer of the *Miracles de Notre-Dame de Rocamadour* [Miracles of Our Lady of Rocamadour] expresses it remarkably well, when he relates the extraordinary case of a woman pregnant for thirty months who, every day, without ever giving birth, is stricken with the pains of labor:

> In this poor wretch, he writes, were fulfilled too well those words which were spoken to the woman in the first days, "You will give birth in pain."[18]

Thus, this suffering also had an ideological function. It recalled the Fall (Genesis 3) and implicitly obliged the Christian to remember his sinful state. It also permitted the woman to participate in her own redemption. If the theme of expiatory suffering for women in labor predates Christianity, the Church made great use of it to call to mind the biblical message.

As the pangs of childbirth ended, the young mother, considered impure, was, in theory, marginalized from Christian society during a period over the course of which a whole group of prohibitions weighed upon her. At the beginning of the seventh century, Pope Gregory the Great writes of it this way to Augustine:

> When a woman has given birth, the number of days after which she can return to the church, you can learn from the Old Testament, that is, thirty-three days for a child of the masculine sex, and sixty-six days for a child of the feminine sex. . . .[19]

This period of isolation for the young mother was never officially prescribed by the Church. However, in practice, it usually lasted about a month and a half, after which the woman, in the image of Mary who waited forty days before presenting Jesus to the Temple, was reintegrated into the Church by a ceremony of purification.

Since the high Middle Ages, contrary to the generally accepted notion that attributes this innovative idea to Jean-Jacques Rousseau, maternal breast-feeding was always valued and preferable to hiring a wet-nurse. Again, it was a means for the mother to redeem herself, in imitating Mary, shown as the Virgin nursing the Child (*Virgo lactans*).

Thus, the Church proposed a rereading and a reinterpretation of maternity, by granting much value to the rites surrounding birth. And thus, it assured the promotion of the mother and the child.

The Struggle against Contraception

Nature, divine in essence, is necessarily good. Thus, the Church opposes all processes which try to thwart it. Did the society of the high Middle Ages follow these precepts to the letter? If it is true that the ancient methods of contraception are less often vouched for, they do not, for all that, disappear. At the beginning of the sixth century, Césaire d'Arles denounces these practices.[20] Penitence rituals inform us of magical potions which certain women took to avoid becoming pregnant. At the beginning of the eleventh century, Burchard de Worms asks, "Have you done as many women do, they take precautions so as not to conceive . . . with evil spells (*maleficia*) and herbs?" The punishment was particularly severe, as he recommends seven years of penitence, the same as for a homicide.[21] Herman, the abbot of Saint Martin de Tournai, evokes the countess Clémence, wife of the count of Flanders, Robert II (1087–1111), who

> after having had three sons by her husband, the count Robert, in the space of three years, feared that if she had still more of them, they would be swept into a struggle over Flanders. So she carried out the feminine procedures (*arte mulierbri*) for having no more children, incurring divine vengeance, because all her sons died long before she did.[22]

As the abbot tells it, the point of this story is to condemn such practices and to warn those who might wish to engage in them that they risk punishment by God. But it makes clear to us as well that, in aristocratic circles, wives, no doubt strongly encouraged by their husbands, tried to limit the number of descendants so that their inheritance would not be spread too thin.

It is important, however, to qualify this idea of widespread contraception in the high Middle Ages. Relying on imprecise knowledge, these practices were not very effective. We will have to wait until the twelfth century for Greco-Roman and Arab contraceptive methods to spread throughout the West, thanks to translations done in Toledo. But, even with these contributions, it is a good bet that the great majority of men and women in the Middle Ages had hardly any effective means of birth control. So what other means of limiting the number of children remained at a couple's disposal? On the one hand, forbidden practices: coitus interruptus, methods considered to go against nature, etc. On the other hand, a sexual hygiene encouraged by the Church: respect for the prohibitions and continence. Jean-Louis Flandrin has shown that in the high Middle Ages a couple who scrupulously respected all the directives imposed by the Church would have had sexual relations only about three days per month.[23]

The Struggle against Abortion

Moreover, Judeo-Christian religion introduces a fundamental notion. Relying upon the fifth commandment, it glorifies life in all its forms, which results in the repeated condemnations of abortion methods in all the capitularies, council canons, and penitence rituals of the high Middle Ages. Such formulas were considered *maleficia*, the products of magic: the seeds of fern or ginger, willow leaves, rue leaves, mixtures of aloes, parsley, fennel, colocynth, or chamomile baths.

The prescriptive texts of the high Middle Ages always take a severe stance toward abortion. However, two criteria modify the penalties incurred by those who willingly interrupt a pregnancy: the context of the conception and the age of the fetus. Indeed, the lawmaker always makes a clear distinction between the woman who has acted out of the worst destitution, for whom condemnation is less harsh, and the fornicator seeking to conceal her crime, who is judged more severely. In 524, the Council of Lerida imposed seven years of excommunication on those who attempted to kill a child resulting from an adulterous affair, either *in utero* or at birth.

The lawmaker also took the estimated time of pregnancy into account. For example, we can read in the penitence rites attributed to Bede (seventh century):

> The mother who kills the child which she carries in her womb before the fortieth day after conception will fast for one year, and after the fortieth day, for three years.[24]

That is to say, for nearly as long a time as for the homicide of a layman (four years). These measures were resumed in the penitence rites of the following centuries, when it seems as though the penalties were increased (up to twelve years of fasting). The severity clearly increases when the child is granted a soul (*animatum*): forty to forty-five days for boys and eighty to ninety days for girls. But this distinction remained theoretical. In practice, it is clear that no one in this epoch was capable of detecting a pregnancy so early on, which, at the same time, limited the effectiveness of abortion methods.

The Repression of Infanticide

In Canon 17 of the Council of Toledo (589), it reads:

> Clerics and civil judges must unite their efforts to destroy this abominable and very widespread practice of parents killing their children in order not to have to feed them.[25]

"Very widespread"? As with abortion, these repeated condemnations do not necessarily translate into very common practices. The council canon, the sentence from the penitence code, the passage from a chronicle are always only distantly related to reality. It is often a matter of a stereotype. Infanticide is the defining mark of bad parents, *par excellence*. By the same token, when clerics described pagan peoples, they made them into child massacrers, even to the point of portraying them wrenching infants from mothers' arms. They were less interested in describing a reality than in reminding the reader of a Christian message. The barbarians were likened to the executioners sent by Herod to kill the newborns. Thus, the cruelty resulting in the murder of children amounted to true genocide, since even the most innocent beings making up the generation which should have continued the race were exterminated. To kill only the adult males, that constituted a "good war." To massacre the women and children as well, that was an attack upon the entire race. If, in the first centuries of the Middle Ages, infanticide was often a crime ascribed to pagans, by the late Middle Ages, it was frequently the Jews who were accused of killing small children and drinking their blood.

However, in this particularly troubled period, destitute parents, being hardly able to feed themselves, sometimes endangered the life of a fetus or a newborn, even if it was often impossible to point to a willful act of negligence. Many councils condemn those parents who suffocated their children by sharing a bed with them or those whose careless supervision led to fatal accidents.

What is especially important and shows how greatly the child was valued is the seriousness of the condemnations leveled against infanticidal parents. At the beginning of the ninth century, the second diocesan statute of Théodulphe d'Orléans condemns a mother who willfully kills her child to exclusion from the church for forty days (as if she had just given birth to it). She must wait four years to be admitted for prayers and ten years to receive the sacrament of communion. But there again, the lawmakers often make distinctions. They do not judge the crime of killing a child who has been baptized as severely as the murder of a non-baptized child, because the latter has not only been assassinated in this world, but is dead for eternity. They also make exceptions for destitute women, whose penalties are much less severe than for others. A text from the end of the eighth century portrays one of these poor women. In about 780, in the village of Bischofheim, near a monastery directed by Saint Lioba, a poor pregnant woman, listed in the charity register of the convent, decides to hide her condition and pretends to be sick. She delivers in secret, wraps the baby in rags, and throws it into a reservoir that the peasants use as a water supply for their mill. Discovering the newborn, a woman immediately accuses the nuns of the monastery. She cries:

> What a chaste congregation, what glorious virginity for these girls who secretly have children and who act as mother and priest at the same time by baptizing the little ones that they bring into the world!

She alerts all the villagers, who "see the sacrilege, shake with horror before the crime, consider the nuns an abomination." The abbess Lioba learns of the affair, assembles the nuns, and notices that one of them is missing, Agatha, who is soon accused of the crime. In the church, before the entire village community, Lioba invokes the judgment of God, and immediately, the poor woman confesses her sin and those present praise the miracle performed by God at the abbess' request.[26]

To its credit, this text shows us the doubts which threaten the respect for the cloister, but more importantly, it informs us of the obvious causes of infanticide, nearly always motivated by the most profound destitution.[27]

Sometimes, returning to a practice which evidence shows to be widespread in antiquity, infanticide is prompted by an infant's deformity. We know, for example, that at the end of the ninth century, the father of Saint Odile tried to kill his daughter, born blind, obliging her mother to hide her for a year in order to protect her from death.

Thus, if infanticide is a reality in the high Middle Ages, it is not at all a widespread phenomenon. It is clear that in most cases, poor women preferred to try to abandon children, hoping they would be adopted by others. Consequently, if the repressive policy of the Church had some effect, it was to favor abandonment.

Abandonment

Abandonment. Was it as common in the Middle Ages as it seems from what is said or written about it?[28] Without claiming to answer this question, we can say that in the difficult periods of the Middle Ages (especially up until the tenth century and in the late Middle Ages) it was a matter of the most Christian solution for parting with a child which you could not raise. Motivated by a powerful respect for life, and facing abject poverty, certain couples were no doubt forced to abandon their children.

In 529, the Council of Vaison stipulated that:

> Whoever finds one of these children must acquire a certificate from the Church and then take it in. Nevertheless, the following Sunday, the priest will announce from the altar that a child has been taken in by a member of the church, so that its parents can reclaim it, if, in the ten days while it is being shown, they can prove that they recognize it. They can give what they wish for the charity offered during those ten days, or leave compensation to the grace of God. If someone's claims or slander worry those who, according to these conditions, would take in the found child, it will be likened to homicide.

The Church Fathers, and lawmakers after them, legitimized abandonment practiced by the most destitute and actively encouraged parents who had no other options to give up one of their children by leaving them in public places so they could more easily be found. In 581, the Council of Mâcon exhorted women to leave children "at the door of the church instead, so that, having been presented to the priest the following day, it [the child] can be taken in and raised by one of the faithful."

In the conciliar decrees compiled in about 906 by Réginon, the abbot of Prüm, whose object was to increase the jurisdiction of the synods, it reads:

> We advise all the priests to announce publicly to their parishioners that if a woman must conceive and give birth following a clandestine union, she certainly must not kill her son or daughter . . . but rather carry the baby to the doors of the church and leave it there, so that it can be brought to the priest in the morning and one of the faithful can take it in and raise it.[29]

According to John Boswell, if the Christian elite began to criticize abandonment, it was less to emphasize the parents' duty to love and educate their child than it was to raise ethical considerations: the mortal risks to which infants were exposed and especially, the fear of involuntary incestuous relations between the child and the "adoptive" parent.[30]

Adoption

In antiquity, kinship could be manipulated thanks to divorce and adoption. In the high Middle Ages, these latter had not disappeared, even if the Church already opposed them. Many cases of adoption are recorded among the Merovingians. In 577, when King Gontran adopted Childebert II, his seven-year-old nephew, he solemnly proclaimed, "It has happened that, because of my sins, I have remained childless, and that is why I ask that this nephew be as a son for me. . . ."[31] This formulation is interesting, because it shows that the ancient practice of adoption was made Christian in the high Middle Ages. When in 585 Childebert, the nephew, came of age, this adoption was given final confirmation, as he was made heir. He then repeated this method of gaining heirs when, a few years later, he in turn adopted his nephew, Gondovald, given up by his father. When his mother presents him, she says to Childebert, "Here is your nephew, son of King Clotaire, and, as he is detested by his father, receive him, because he is your flesh." Gregory of Tours adds, "Receiving him because he had no son, he [Childebert] takes him into his home."[32]

In these two cases, adoption is paired with a blood tie, as if this method of filiation were a compromise between adopting a complete stranger and a natural relative. It is a matter of legitimizing a member of the family already linked by blood to the adoptive father. However, it also happens that adoptions take place outside of the family. Sigebert III, for example, Merovingian king from 633 to 656, had no children and, pressured by his Grimoald mayor, he adopted a son from him who, to bind himself to the Merovingian dynasty, took the name of Childebert, the traditional anthroponym of the Merovingians. "Childebert l'Adopté" reigned from 656 to 662. In this case, adoption was used as a tool by which the palace mayors could gradually assert their power in the face of the descendants of Clovis. It foreshadows, a century beforehand, the "*coup d' état*" of Pépin le Bref, which resulted in a change in the dynasty in control of Gaul.

In eighth-century Spain, we encounter cases of legal adoption which provide for a remuneration to be given to the adoptive family:

> If someone accepts a child from its parents in order to raise it, he can demand a price of one *solidus* per year, every year until the child is ten years old. After which, there is nothing more to pay since the child is able to work to provide for itself.[33]

Within the framework of the terrible anti-Jewish measures adopted by the councils of Toledo, the Visigoths even ordered Jewish children to be taken from their parents and placed in Christian homes.[34] Across the Channel, adoption existed legally. The term "*fostermoder*" (fostermother), found very frequently in Anglo-Saxon literature from the high Middle Ages, undoubtedly refers more to a surrogate mother than to a wet nurse.[35]

It was especially at the beginning of the Carolingian period that divorce and adoption became difficult for men in high places, as the western Church gradually succeeded in prohibiting and controlling the means of manipulating kinship. We know, for example, all the difficulties encountered by Lothaire II of Lotharingie in the middle of the ninth century, in his efforts to divorce his sterile wife and remarry his mistress by whom he already had children. This legal-canonical barrier does not prevent the existence of "informal adoption" in the centuries that follow, resulting from the death of parents, abandonment, parental separation, putting children in a nurse's care, fosterage*, or putting children to work.

TWO

The Christian Child

The Age of Innocence

The innocence of the child is not a new idea. But Christian intellectuals, relying on the New Testament, never stopped insisting upon this theme throughout the Middle Ages. "See that you do not despise a single one of these little
ones, because, I tell you, in heaven, their angels remain forever in the presence of
my Father who is in heaven" (Matthew 18:10). The biblical text insists as well on
the necessity of being like a little child in order to enter paradise. "In truth I tell
you, whoever does not receive the Kingdom of God as a little child will not enter
there" (Mark 10:15 and Luke 18:17).

Exploring the question of the child coming to symbolize humility in the
New Testament (Matthew 18:3–4), Saint Jerome presents the child as an exemplary being which God has sent to earth. He praises the young for experiencing no pleasure with regard to women, for not concealing their thoughts, for
not lying, for not persisting in their anger, and for not remembering the offenses
of others against them.[1] And Leon the Great, pope from 440 to 461, going even
further, adds, "Christ loves childhood, mistress of humility, rule of innocence,
model of gentleness. . . . He gives it as an example to all those He raises to the
eternal realm."[2]

In monastic writings, three qualities are always praised in the child, which
a monk must devote himself to regaining: innocence, humility, and purity. Moreover, in the *Etymologies*, Isidore of Seville explains that the word *puer* comes from
puritas: "They are called *pueri* because of their purity."[3] Beginning from the ninth
century, illuminators represent all very small children nude to extol their innocence and purity. A miniature for the psalter of Utrecht (about 820) represents a
mother holding a newborn by the arms in the air, which illustrates Psalm 85:12:
"Truth will spring from the ground."[4] These constant references to childlike
innocence as exemplary Christian virtue are not limited to monastic circles.
The two children of Queen Ethelberga of Northumbria, sent to Gaul to the court
of King Dagobert out of concern for their safety, "both died in early youth and

21

were buried in the church, with all the honors rendered to the children of kings and to the innocent children of Christ."[5]

From the first centuries of the Middle Ages, both in art and in literature, the theme of the Massacre of the Innocents was developed and continued to be enormously successful throughout the entire course of the medieval period. A few days after Christmas (December 28), the day of the Innocents was celebrated. Beginning from the eleventh century, chapels were built to them and some of their relics were even discovered, as at the abbey of Brogne in 1116. With much feeling, artists described the poignant reactions of the mothers from whom the slaughterers, under orders from Herod, seized babies. These widespread images conveyed the strong attachment of parents to their children, the innocence of the very young, and their sympathy with Christ, since not only were these children of Bethlehem, less than two years old—the first martyrs of the Christian religion—massacred unjustly *for Christ*, but they died *in the place of Christ*. That is why theologians gradually accepted the dogma according to which these infants were saved by their suffering and the blood they spilled, even though they were not baptized.

The Infans* Made Sacred

Christianity grafted itself to a world in the midst of profound religious change—that is also what explains its rapid success—in which the sacred was becoming evermore present. The new religion intensified this obsessive search for purity, defined, first of all, as a distancing from things of the flesh. Within this context, the *infans* very soon appears to be a profoundly sacred being who, in many ways, recalls the son of God: baptism can only be received a single time, because it is given in the death of Christ. To rebaptize is to crucify Jesus again. In the ninth century, for example, Amalaire de Metz asks that baptism take place at the ninth hour, because that was the hour when Christ breathed his last.[6] Some parents bring their deaf-mute infant to the Saint Martin de Tours basilica where he is placed on a small bed. Martin appears to the bishop Gregory of Tours and says to him, "Have the lamb leave the basilica, because he is healed."[7] The lamb, we know, is the ultimate image of Christ who comes to save humanity. At the moment when they raise the host, often monks will see a very small child appear in it, just as it is also common for the soul to be represented by an *infans* in art, as, for example, when it withdraws from the body of the Virgin at the time of death or, again, in the bosom of Abraham.

God makes the infant a key figure in intercession. The hagiographers recount miracles in the course of which an *infans* comes to reveal a message to men through a laugh or a word. In the ninth century, for example, the bishop of Trêves wanted to put Saint Goar to the test. He asked him to make an infant, abandoned three days after birth, speak and so reveal his parentage. The infant then declaimed that the bishop was his father.[8] In the manner of angels, the young child appears in dreams to transmit divine directives. In England at the end of the twelfth century, Richard, an adolescent, had been very ill for nine years, and no one knew how to cure him. It is his newborn brother who tells him to go to the tomb of Thomas Becket to recover his health.[9]

Also, sometimes a very young child was asked to open the Bible at random. The verse at which it fell open would then be taken as a prophecy. In the middle of the fifth century, at the time of a very difficult decision regarding the choice of a bishop of Orléans, the name of the future Saint Aignan was chosen by an infant, not yet able to talk (*necdum loquens*), but suddenly granted oratorical capacities just for this occasion.[10] At the end of the twelfth century, Jean de Salisbury tells how, when he was an infant, his master used him and his little comrades to do divinations. He would coat their fingernails with holy oils and make them read in a cooking pot.[11]

Implicitly or explicitly, the clergy who presented these stories referred to the Bible. "Oh God, our Lord, how great is your name on all the earth! Above the heavens, how your majesty is chanted by the mouths of babes, of infants" (Psalms 8:2–3). And this is taken up again in Matthew, when Jesus chases the vendors from the Temple: "Out of the mouth of babes and infants, you have brought forth praise" (Matthew 21:16).

Likewise, small children are the special beneficiaries of divine visions. We know, for example, that in 1178, Christ appeared to Benoît (Benezet), still a small child then, during a solar eclipse, and ordered him to build a bridge across the Rhône—the famous bridge of Avignon.[12]

Adolescents

The very young child occupied a special place in Christian thinking. The same thing was not true for the adolescent. Christian intellectuals exhibited great anxiety concerning this period of life. Julien de Vézeley writes:

> After childhood comes adolescence, a sensual and undisciplined age which believes that virtue is tiresome and difficult, and which is keen on pleasure. The sensual delight of perverse attractions teases at the still-naive soul, and if it succeeds in taking hold of it, it defiles it with shameful vices. [Adolescence is] unstable, it doesn't let itself be guided by reason or by the advice of others, but, subject to the whim of various temptations, it lets itself be led here and there, moving about restlessly. One day, it wants to, the next day, it doesn't want to. Today it loves something, tomorrow, it hates it.[13]

That summarizes the principal qualities attributed to the adolescent. He had an unstable disposition, was undisciplined, careless, sensual, had no taste for effort, and delighted in pleasure. In narrative texts, he is often presented as a person inclined toward excess, with a tendency for overreacting and blasphemous speech. In his autobiography from the beginning of the twelfth century, Guibert de Nogent evokes this age when he lacked self-restraint and was subject to his impulses. "Thus, while my young body grew little by little, my soul was also aroused by worldly life, titillated in its own right by sexual desires and lust."[14]

With regard to female adolescents, accounts are rarer and more ambiguous. Actually, the dawning of female sexuality was even more disquieting to the clerics in that it recalls the reason for the Fall. However, particularly in the accounts of miracles, young girls are very positive figures because of their chastity and their virginity.[15] We know of the example of Agnes, the twelve-year-old martyr of the very first centuries A.D., who quickly became a model for the hagiographers of the centuries that followed. Wisdom has it that she ascended to heaven and received two crowns from God, one for her martyrdom and one for her virginity. These are also the qualities which allow female adolescents to be the frequent beneficiaries of visions which reveal divine messages. Like small children, they played a role in "deciphering the beyond." When the "ghost of Beaucaire," Guillaume, shows himself to the living from July to September 1211, it is to his cousin, a young virgin of eleven years, that he appears. He says to her, "It is to you alone that I am allowed to speak, and it is through you alone that I am allowed to transmit my responses to the others." For two months, neighbors come to see the young girl and ask questions to the dead "through the mouth of the little girl." The ghost explains to his cousin that if she loses her virginity, he will never appear to her again.[16]

The great value placed on young girls was a way of recalling Mary's virginity, as the great value given to infants allowed the Infant Jesus to be seen and seen again. But, we must qualify this very positive view of childhood in the high Middle Ages.

Some Harsh Judgments of the Child

A negative image of the child undeniably existed, which originated in ancient tradition and in the Old Testament (Proverbs 22:15 and Book of Wisdom 12:24). We are familiar with the famous words of Saint Augustine, in his *Confessions*, from the beginning of the fifth century: "what is innocent about the child is the weakness of his bodily organs, but not his soul."[17] His lack of autonomy is the perfect image of human dependence with regard to God. However, the negative judgments always emanated from those who did not have children and who were not familiar with them, the clergy. They rejected them, just as they condemned all that belonged to this world and disrupted meditation or the life of the intellect. Let us think, for example, of the arguments Héloïse uses to try to dissuade Abélard from marrying her:

> Is there a man who, devoted to meditating upon the Scriptures and philosophy, can bear the wails of the newborn, the songs of the nurse who consoles it, the constant grubbiness of young children?[18]

Every birth recalls original sin. For Saint Augustine, "no one is free of sin before You [God], not even the little infant who has lived on the earth only one day."[19] At the beginning of the eighth century, to refute the opinions of the Pelagians, the Venerable Bede writes:

as for men, they are all born marked by original sin, and it is known that they bear the mark of the fall of Adam, even if they live sinlessly now, according to the words of the prophet: "Thus I am born in iniquity; I was sinful in the womb of my mother."[20]

Thus, to erase this stain transmitted to the child by its parent by heredity and to obtain a chance for salvation, there was only one solution: baptism. As the New Testament affirms, "Without being born of water and the Spirit, no one can enter the kingdom of God" (John 3:5).

Baptism of Small Children

Baptism is, at once, the sacramental ritual which washes away original sin and the social ceremony which integrates a person into the Christian community. Already, canonical texts and rites of penitence from the high Middle Ages recommend baptizing an infant very soon after birth. In general, they fix three years as the maximum age for receiving this sacrament. To better mark the direct link which exists between the rite of baptism, a veritable second birth, and the Resurrection of Christ, they recommend that the ceremony take place during the most important times for the Christian calendar, the Saturdays of Easter and Pentecost which are reserved at first for the catechumen.* In 585, the second canon of the Council of Mâcon strongly recommends that henceforth, baptism be conferred in all of Merovingian Gaul only on Easter Saturday. Chilpéric, the Merovingian king, had his son baptized at Easter by the bishop Ragnemod.[21] Paul Diacre, too, informs us that Adaloald, the very young son of the Lombard king, Agilulf, was baptized at Saint-Jean de Monza on Easter Sunday.[22] The same author relates the destruction of the town of Forlimpopoli (in Tuscie) by the king of the Lombards, Grimoald:

> He attacked the town without warning right in the middle of Easter Saturday, a very sacred day, at the time of the baptisms, and left such a harvest of bodies, killing even the deacons who baptized the little children, right at the sacred fountain.[23]

Charlemagne gave great importance to baptism, which became not only an instrument for converting the pagans, but also the veritable cement of the Carolingian empire, composed of so many diverse peoples. About 811–812, the emperor sent a very detailed questionnaire to all the metropolitans of his empire, to learn about the baptismal rituals of each province. We still have some of the responses. We learn from them that children were baptized very soon after birth, because the parental anguish over seeing babies die unbaptized was growing increasingly great. In England in the same period, civil and religious law required that baptism take place before children were one month old.

But pedobaptism*—that is, immediately after birth—was far from common before the seventh–eighth centuries, even within the most Christian circles of high aristocracy. At the end of the ninth century, Saint Odile was baptized more than a year after her birth and Saint Vincent of Saint-Viance, at two years.[24] The practice of baptizing at Easter did not disappear. We know, for example, that on Holy Saturday, 853, when the Normans burst into the cathedral in Nantes, they killed the bishop who was in the process of baptizing infants. Canon 7 of the 829 Council of Paris, and Canon 3 of the 847 Council of Mayence indicate that baptisms would only be performed at Easter and Pentecost unless necessity required otherwise.

The widespread practice of pedobaptism would require modification of the baptismal rite. Examinations, which consisted of asking the person being baptized to recite the *Pater* and the *Credo*, or to respond to certain questions from the priest, in order to verify his or her knowledge of the religion, would disappear. They were gradually replaced by exorcisms, accompanied by signs of the cross and prayers. On the other hand, it became necessary henceforth for the adults to make a commitment in the name of the child: "if it is a matter of small children, those who respond for them are forgiven in the name of the faith."[25] Christening, no doubt, predates the development of pedobaptism, but the latter could only reinforce the former. Henceforth, spiritual kinship would become essential, since it reminded the faithful that divine filiation was superior to biological filiation, and it played an important role in washing away the sins of the flesh. According to the Church, the godfather and godmother were to take charge of the religious education of the child, and be moral supervisors for their godchild to help secure his or her salvation. Finally, the expansion of pedobaptism led to the gradual transition from immersion in the baptismal font to a pouring or sprinkling of holy water. But this change occurred very slowly and synodical statutes from the thirteenth century still called for triple immersion.

The Ceremony of Baptism

Administered by the priest, baptism was only performed in baptismal churches, and not in just any parish church. It was to be free of charge, even if the administering priest could accept gifts. First, at the church entrance, the parish priest questioned the godparents who gave him the child's chosen first name. Often, the child had to wait until this solemn moment to be officially named. We know, for example, that in the ninth century, the second son of the aristocrat, Dhuoda, bore no name, because he was not yet baptized.[26] In aristocratic Frankish circles in the high Middle Ages, a son was nearly always given one of the names used in his maternal or paternal family, often that of his grandfather. In other circles, there is evidence for the onomastic practice of modeling the names of children on those of the father and/or the mother. For example, in the polyptych* of Saint-Germain-des-Prés (813), the children of Aldaldus are named Aldoardus and Aldoildis.

After receiving the name, the priest pronounced many exorcism formulas, proceeded to the laying on of hands, then to the symbolic opening of the seats of the senses (the *epheta*), and to anointing the chest and the shoulders. These recitations were meant to prepare the child for receiving baptism and to expel the demon:

> "Do you renounce Satan, and all his pomp and vanities, and all his works?"
> The spiritual parents respond for the child:
> "I renounce Satan, and all his pomp and vanities, and all his work . . . and all the known spirits."
> Then the interrogation directed toward the symbol:
> "Do you believe in the almighty God the Father?"
> "I believe in the almighty God the Father."
> "Do you believe in Christ the son of God?"
> "I believe. . . ."
> "Do you believe in the Holy Spirit?"
> "I believe. . . ."[27]

Then, all the participants entered the church, where the child was taken to the baptismal font by his spiritual parents. He was then immersed or sprinkled three times, the gesture accompanied by the words: "I baptize you in the name of the Father, of the Son and of the Holy Ghost." Beginning from this moment, the child was Christian. If he died, his acknowledged state of great innocence and purity allowed him to ascend to paradise. On the other hand, if he died before having received baptism, in the high Middle Ages, he went to hell.

The Child Who Dies Unbaptized

Following the quarrel with the Pelagians at the beginning of the fifth century, Saint Augustine condemned dead unbaptized children to hell. This theological position remained unchanged until at least the twelfth century. It was very widely held. For example, about 830, Jonas d'Orléans writes:

> Now that the name of Christ is strongly proclaimed throughout and children are born of Christian parents, it is necessary that they be presented without delay to receive the gift of baptism, even if they do not yet speak. We are right to do this so that these children, guilty of the sins of others, be absolved of their participation in original sin by the actions and the responses of others, and thus be lifted from the power of darkness, to enter the kingdom of their Lord.[28]

In a letter addressed to Hincmar de Reims, in about 850, Loup de Ferrières writes this with regard to newborns:

> if they die after having received the gift of baptism, they are saved by the will of God; on the other hand, deprived by God's judgment of this very gift of baptism, they are damned by the fault of the hereditary sin committed by the will of the father.[29]

Dead without baptism, the child was called *paganus*. Their fate in the beyond was similar to that of pagans. They were not allowed Christian burials. The parents who, out of negligence, delayed having children baptized, and thus conspired to close the doors of heaven to them, were more and more severely condemned, between one and seven years of penitence according to the councils and penitence codes. The priest who delayed in coming was dismissed from his duties. Sometimes the parents were even strongly encouraged to give this sacrament themselves, especially in cases when infants were in danger of dying.

Thus, we can understand the terrible anguish of parents at the brutal death of a baby not yet baptized, as is evident in this example of a woman who had just lost her son, as recounted by Gregory of Tours. "The mother cried not so much over the death of her infant as over the fact that he had not yet received the divine sacrament of baptism."[30] But there is no doubt that, from the high Middle Ages on, parents were not satisfied with this doctrinal position which they considered unjust. In Provence, a parental epitaph was found, dating from the sixth century, on the tomb of an infant named Theodose de la Gayole. This inscription indicates that the child had been "provided with the rampart of the cross, innocent, saved from the filth of sin . . . his parents, with pure intentions, wished to see him plunged in the sacred baptism of water." This epitaph demonstrates the parents' attempt, in any case, to persuade themselves that their infant was saved, thanks to their intentions to baptize him.

The belief in "respite" miracles is an illustration of parental refusal to think of their progeny as damned. In this type of miracle, the saint or the Virgin intervenes to bring a dead unbaptized child back to life for the time needed to administer the sacrament in order to avoid eternal damnation. In the high Middle Ages, there is no lack of examples of this. In a sermon, Saint Augustine reports one of the first cases of respite known, attributed to Saint Etienne. A woman of Uzale, in Africa, hurries up to the blessed martyr Etienne, with her small, dead, unbaptized infant, and, in tears, implores the saint to bring him back to life. The infant revives. Immediately, he is carried to the priests and baptized, after which time, he dies.[31] This example is seminal, creating a model for the hagiographers.

At the beginning of the eighth century, a child still at the breast dies. His mother, learning that the bishop Wilfrid of York is making his rounds in the diocese to confirm the children, brings her dead son, trying to make believe that he is still alive, so that he can "escape the jaws of the lion." But Saint Wilfrid notices. At the express request of the mother, he revives the child for a time and baptizes him to ensure his eternal salvation.[32] In 1160, in Arras, along the shores of the Grinchon, a walker hears something fall into the water. He sees that it is a little girl and alerts the neighborhood. The child is fished out. The mother recognizes her daughter "already stiff and cold, without speech or feeling." She runs to the neighboring church, Sainte-Marie-au-Jardinet, and places the child on the altar, pleading in tears and in prayers for her resurrection, and the miracle happens.[33] The respite can take place in a sanctuary, and it does not have to be a special one as would be the case after the fourteenth century.

Beginning at the end of the twelfth century, dead unbaptized infants were gradually granted a new status and new place in the hereafter: limbo for children (*limbus puerorum*). There, they were forever deprived of the beatific vision (to which every Christian aspired), but they escaped the torments of hell.[34]

Rights to the Sacraments

After baptism, the young Christian in the Middle Ages still had to undergo a certain number of rites and ceremonies. First, he had to confirm the commitment that his spiritual parents made for him at the time of baptism. At the beginning of Christianity, the ceremony of confirmation was associated with that of baptism. Then, largely because baptism was performed on younger and younger children, it gradually became disassociated over the course of the sixth to eighth centuries, and, in the twelfth to thirteenth century, it was required that the child attain the age of reason, that is, seven years, before being confirmed. At the same time, confirmation became monopolized by the bishop. Even if, as Ruotger de Trêves specifies in the early tenth century, it was "very dangerous" for a baptized but unconfirmed child to die, because he had not received the full Christian faith,[35] confirmation was not considered indispensable for salvation. It was carried out by two essential gestures which were meant to impart the Holy Spirit to the child: the laying on of hands and a sign on the forehead made with the chrism, or holy oil. But this rite was, doubtlessly, seldom performed. The majority of Christians, out of negligence or lack of interest, did not take their children to be confirmed.

The child becomes still a bit more integrated into the community of the faithful through confession and communion. In the fourth and fifth centuries, very young children were admitted to communion. The custom then was to have them receive communion, at least the wine, which was often not consecrated, at the time of their baptism. Under the Carolingians, this practice tended to disappear. The 813 Council of Tours forbids giving children communion "indiscreetly." It was not until 1215, with Canon 21 (*omnis utriusque sexus*) of the Latran IV Council, that the Church would require all children past "the age of discretion" (in this canon, seven years, no doubt), to confess their sins at least once a year, and receive "at least at Easter, the sacrament of the Eucharist."[36]

The Child in the Cemetery

In the many necropolises from the Merovingian period, we can note a very clear under-representation in the number of individuals younger than eighteen to twenty years old (between 3 and 30 percent of all the individuals exhumed) and the almost total absence of skeletons of newborns and young babies. In Lower Normandy, for example, in the cemeteries of Verson, Sannerville, Frénouville, and Giberville-le-Martray, no child from the sixth century less than four years old has been identified. Thus, the rarity of remains of infants in the cemeteries does not reflect the demographic reality at all. In the Carolingian period, on the other hand, in rural as well as urban centers, there is a "conquest of the community cemetery by the little children."[37] These latter are, indeed, more numerous, coming close to the actual demographics.

The interpretation of these facts is a delicate matter. Where were infants buried prior to the eighth century? And what accounts for the emergence of dead infants in the necropolises beginning from the start of the Carolingian period? Is it connected with the evangelization of the rural world and how deeply Christian society had become, characterized by parishes multiplying and rustic cemeteries situated far from communities being abandoned for new cemeteries established in the center of the village, near the church? The missing children: are they the ones who were not baptized? We must be very careful in answering these questions. In the Merovingian period, the cemetery did not have the status it would be given beginning from the tenth century when it became a holy place, blessed and sacred. The idea of excluding non-Christians from this place did not yet have any very clear meaning.[38] Moreover, as we have seen, infant baptism was widespread enough that we would expect to find many children in the cemeteries.

Perhaps, with or without baptism, because of the general recognition of their faultless character, they were buried elsewhere, nearer to home. For the very early Middle Ages (and up until the eleventh century), children's—and frequently babies'—tombs have been found, in fact, outside of cemeteries, within or very near dwelling places. It seems clear, in any case, that before the Carolingian period, the right to burial in community cemeteries was rarely, if ever, extended toward children.

Within the cemetery, are children's tombs located in a particular place? It is difficult to answer this question, as it is often the case that archaeologists cannot identify an entire cemeterial site, and, as a result, many remains escape their study. Beginning from the Merovingian epoch, as long as we are not very systematic about it, we can notice areas in the necropolises in which there is a very heavy concentration of young children (often young babies and newborns), sometimes at the periphery of the cemetery, sometimes beside a religious building, under the rain gutter (sub stillicidio) in order to benefit from the good effects of the purifying waters which run off the roof of the building. In the village of Saint-Martin de Trainecourt, at Mondeville in the Calvados, there are 430 burial sites of which 106 are for children, often very young children, located in the north-northwest area of the cemetery, in particular along the wall marking the limit of the space for graves.[39] In La Courneuve, the excavations of the Saint-Lucien church show that 85 percent of the tombs discovered along the southern extension of the building are those of children.[40] Around the Saint-Barthélemy church, beside the basilica of Saint-Denis, a majority of young children are buried near the south wall of church chancel, beginning from the ninth century. In the necropolis of the Cour d'Albane, the episcopal group of Rouen (tenth and eleventh centuries), 30 percent of the non-adult interments are located along the south wall of Saint-Etienne church, always under the rain gutters. In this sector, nearly 30 percent of the children's graves are for infants less than a year old. A great number of children are also found in the nave of the Saint-Etienne church (68 percent of the remains in this area) and, notably, in the entrance. Among them, more than a quarter are newborns and two thirds are less than ten years old. This location at the entrance can be associated with the presence of the baptismal fonts, very often situated in the northwestern part of the church, and with Saint Etienne, whose special duty it is to protect and resurrect stillborn infants.[41]

At Dassargues, between Nîmes and Montpellier, for the Carolingian period, children from one to six years old are buried in an area at the periphery of the necropolis. As for the newborns, they are never buried in this sector, but are found either in the chevet of the church, under the purifying water which drips from the roof, or in a non-religious place, far from the church and houses (one group of tombs in an area used for silage, and another group in a farm wall). Perhaps we can assume, then, that those in the chevet received baptism and the others did not?[42]

Carefully Prepared Tombs

Children were buried with as much care as adults. The graves were dug to their dimensions, sometimes surrounded with a framework of stones, and covered over with stone slabs. The small corpse was often positioned with the head facing west, laid out on its back, the forearms bent and the hands placed on the pubis. We can note as well that, at least until the beginning of the eighth century, children, like adults, could be buried fully dressed and with various furnishings. The objects and clothes found in their tombs testify to a genuine desire on the part of parents or society to pay homage to the dead young ones and are, no doubt, signs of affection. In the tombs of some barbarian children, figurines, terracotta birds, ivory dolls, tops, and balls have been found. Under the cathedral of Cologne, a tomb of a child dating from the sixth century contained a small chair. A low seat designed for children to use and small dishes filled with hazelnuts have been found in other German graves, the dishes resting on the children's chests. At Saint-Martin-de-Fontenay, the tomb of a newborn, dating from around 765, contained two bronze clasps and an iron chain. In the cemetery of Mondeville in the Calvados (seventh–eighth century) an infant was exhumed bearing two double hooked fasteners of bronze.[43] Near Lunel (between Nîmes and Montpellier) a child about five years old was buried wearing a necklace of amber and glass beads, with keys lying alongside the body.[44] In Lisieux, two young children, one, three years old, and the other, six months, had been buried in the fourth century in lead caskets. The use of such costly metal, imported from Normandy, indicates without a doubt that these were children from privileged social classes. It also attests to a real desire to give these children a burial worthy of the love that they surely received when alive and equal to the grief felt by the parents.

Thus, despite the harshness of the times and the high rate of infant and child mortality, men and women of the Middle Ages took the care and time to attend to their dead children also, to provide them comfort in eternity and to comfort themselves on earth. In life, as in death, children of the high Middle Ages were surrounded with their parents' love, as in this image of a Carolingian baby from the Villiers-le-Sec necropolis, dead at about six months, interred in the pelvis of a man dead at about forty years old.[45]

THREE

Difficult Living Conditions

A Demography of the "Ancient Regime"

Because it was the purpose of marriage, and few effective means of contraception existed, the number of births was very high. Faced with limited sources of information, it is impossible to estimate precisely the fertility and birth rate of the high Middle Ages. The only numbers mentioned regarding children almost always come from aristocratic circles. We know, for example, that the Merovingian king, Clotaire, "has had seven children by various women" and Chilpéric "had at this time four sons born by various women, not to mention his daughters."[1] At the beginning of the seventh century, Romilda, the wife of the duke of Frioul Gisulf found herself a widow with eight children (four sons and four daughters).[2] In twelve years of marriage with Hildegarde, Charlemagne engendered eight children as well.

But parallel to all these births are the many infant deaths. By relying upon much later demographic facts which can, nevertheless, be applied to the medieval period, we can estimate the infant mortality rate (before the age of one) to be on the order of 200 to 400 for 1000. That is to say that, on the average, three children out of ten, born living, died before the end of their first year. Nearly as many died before the age of puberty. Thus, it was scarcely one child out of two who survived to procreate. Those levels of society which we could reasonably imagine offering more favorable living conditions did not escape this devastation: 36 percent of the children engendered by the Carolingian kings of the ninth and tenth centuries did not reach the age of twenty.[3] The attitude of Catalan testators about the year 1000 is completely revealing of how this demographic fact is taken into account. In 1020, for example, at the time of establishing the order of his succession, the count Bernard Taillefer envisioned the death of three of his sons. His contemporary, Ermengol d'Olo, anticipated the possible loss of all his five children.[4]

Thus, in the high Middle Ages, the renewal of generations was always difficult to guarantee. Let us remember that we witness a population decline from the third to the end of the sixth century, and that, in the West, the seventh and eighth centuries correspond to the lowest demographic figures. And the settling of barbarians (not more than 3–4 percent of the population living in the Empire in the sixth century) does little to counteract this fall.

The study of eleventh-century Carolingian polyptychs from the Ile-de-France, Provence, Picardie, and the Champagne region reveal a population characterized by a very real dynamism which was nevertheless unequal and chaotic. It would not be until the eleventh century that, as demographic and economic conditions improved, the population of the West would noticeably increase. The study of a few noble lineages of Namurois, between 1000 and 1250, informs us that, on the average, a couple engendered between 4.30 and 5.75 children who reached adulthood.[5]

Infant mortality was particularly common at birth or in the hours or days immediately following. We know that the queen Faileube, wife of King Chidebert, "gave birth to a stillborn child and that she remained unwell." King Charibert had, by Theudogilde, "a son who was carried to the grave as soon as he left the womb." Just after receiving baptism, Ingomer, the son of Clotilde and Clovis, was "recalled from this world while he was in his white garments, to be provided for under the gaze of God."[6] The king of Northumbria, Edwin, lost a son and a daughter as well "while they still wore their white garments."[7] The king Chilpéric had already lost a number of sons, before Thierry was born, his infant who survived only a year.[8] Archaeological digs corroborate this very high mortality rate. The immature (less than eighteen or twenty years old) represent 40 to 50 percent of the total number of graves excavated in Carolingian necropolises. In the cemetery of Notre-Dame of Cherbourg, for example, in which the majority of graves date from the ninth and tenth centuries, 45 percent of the exhumed population is less than eighteen years old, while those under four years old represent 58 percent of the total of the immature, and 25 percent are infants under a year old. In the cemetery of Villiers-le-Sec, eleven skeletons out of forty-eight (23 percent) are under five years old. At Saint-Victor of Marseille, 22 percent of the children are under twelve. In the cemetery of Mondeville Delle-Saint-Martin (seventh-twelfth centuries), the immature occupy at least 32 percent of the burial sites, and among them, newborns make up a quarter of the total number, and children of ages one to four, 41 percent. When archaeological digs allow more precision, it becomes clear that those most threatened by mortality were apparently babies of less than three months, and next, children of about three years, perhaps more vulnerable because they had just been weaned. Archaeology also indicates that a lull in the death rate occurred especially after ten years, which confirms Philippe de Novare's reflection (thirteenth century): "You know that, from their birth until they have turned ten, children are in too great danger of death and disease."[9]

Diseases

The high infant mortality is explained, first of all, by the lack of hygiene, malnutrition, and the absence of effective medicine. Dysentery and fever were the two principal afflictions which plagued infants. Sanson, the youngest son of the Merovingian king, Chilpéric (577–584), hardly five years old, "having been stricken with dysentery and fever, quit the world of humans,"[10] as did three others of his sons under the same conditions. With much feeling, Gregory of Tours evokes this epidemic of dysentery which caused such terrible loss at the end of the sixth century:

> This malady . . . first attacked children and caused them to perish: we lost our dear sweet little children whom we had cradled at our bosoms, held in our arms, nourished with the greatest care, giving them their food from our own hands.[11]

Accounts of miracles sometimes describe the violent pains which assailed the infants who could no longer eat and rejected all food. Archaeology corroborates this impression given by the texts. Observing the skeletons in the necropolises, one becomes aware of deep lesions, wounds, decalcification, bad teeth, in short, a state of relatively poor health.

Faced with this devastation and the impotence of medicine, the clerics liked to show the power of Christianity as an effective recourse for saving a child from death. We know of the events preceding the baptism of Clovis, at the end of the fifth century, which led to the conversion of the grandson of Mérovée, according to Gregory of Tours. Certainly, there was the famous battle of Tolbiac, but also, immediately before this decisive victory over the Alamans, a less well-known event took place. Clotilde, the wife of Clovis,

> gave birth to another son, who was baptized and who she named Clodomir. Now as he began to be ill, the king [Clovis] said, "The same thing will happen to him as what happened to his brother;[12] baptized in the name of your Christ, he will immediately die."

But, thanks to his mother's prayers, "he was cured by God's order."[13] Again, according to Gregory of Tours, who is always attempting in his work to prove to a still only partially Christian population the real power of God, even receiving baptism is an effective remedy against illness. During the terrible epidemic of dysentery at the end of the sixth century, a son of Chilpéric, "who was not yet reborn by the water and the Holy Spirit, fell sick. When he was on the point of death, he was washed in the water of baptism."[14] And immediately, the child's condition improved.

Plagues, Famines, Violence

To these endogenous causes of mortality are added, at the beginning of the Middle Ages, exogenous causes, especially in the form of epidemics, famines, and physical danger. The second half of the sixth century and the beginning of the seventh century are, indeed, marked by an epidemic of plagues impossible to count but horribly destructive, especially in southern Europe, and leading to grave crises. This is what the pope, Gregory the Great, is supposed to have said with regard to this epidemic, in a public address reported by Gregory of Tours:

> Here we find, indeed, that the whole population is struck with the two-edged sword of heavenly anger and that each individual is the victim of this unforeseen massacre . . . the parents contemplate the funerals of sons and their heirs precede them in death.[15]

Just as they were at the time of the great epidemics and famines of the last medieval centuries, people appeared to be very sensitive to this reversal of the natural order of things, represented by the premature death of children.

In the high Middle Ages, the absence of high-performance tools kept production at a very low level. People produced primarily to subsist. Climatic changes had catastrophic effects on harvests and led very quickly to food shortages. In 1033, the chronicler Raoul Glaber describes the terrible famine which ravaged the Burgundy region, during the course of which children were doubly the victims:

> In the following epoch, the famine began to extend its devastation over all the land and there was reason to fear that the human species might almost entirely disappear. The atmospheric conditions were so unfavorable that a good time could not be found for a single sowing, and, especially because of the floods, there was no means for harvesting. . . . As the shortage of provisions struck the entire population, the affluent and those in the middle class became as gaunt as the poor; the plundering by the powerful had to come to an end in the face of universal destitution. . . . To escape death, some took recourse to the forests for roots and to the rivers for grasses. . . . Alas, a thing rarely heard of through all the ages, raging hunger pushed men to devouring human flesh. Sometimes travelers were carried off by those more robust than they, their limbs severed, roasted over fires, and devoured. Even people going from one place to another to flee the famine, having found a place along the way to rest for the night, would have their throats slit, and be served as food to those who had received them. Many would present eggs or pieces of fruit to children to lure them to isolated spots, and then massacre and devour them. In some places the bodies of the dead were even torn up from the ground and served to appease hunger as well.[16]

The first centuries A.D. were also deeply marked by violence, due as much to migrant barbarian peoples as to the established Romanized populations. In these "Dark Ages," numerous accounts testify to aggressions against the very young. Even if, as we have noted, the crimes perpetrated on children become, for the clergy, a way of further "barbarizing" the pagans, the period of the high Middle Ages is marked by two waves of invasions which claimed children among their victims. We learn, for example, that the Thuringians "hung young boys from the trees by their thighs; they savagely killed more than two hundred young girls."[17] The Venerable Bede mentions that terrible figure, Cadwallon, king of the Bretons, who, backed by Penda, the king of Mercia, eliminated the Christian Edwin in October 633:

> But Cadwallon, although he bore a Christian name and flaunted himself as such, was so barbaric in terms of mind and morals that he spared neither the feminine sex nor the innocence of small defenseless children, but, with savage cruelty, he put them to death, inflicting horrible tortures upon them. . . .[18]

The unity of the *regnum Francorum*, carried out under the aegis of Clovis and his sons, also led to the massacre of children. In 523, Sigismond, king of the Burgondes, was taken prisoner by Clodomir. He was led away in captivity and assassinated with his wife and children by the Merovingian king Clodomir, who then threw them into a well.[19] There are plenty of examples of aristocratic children who, in the fratricidal Merovingian wars of the sixth century, suffered the same fate as their fathers. Childebert, son of Clovis and Clotilde, seeing his mother showing too much affection for her grandchildren (ages ten and seven), the sons of his brother Clodomir, makes him believe that he wants to raise them for the throne, and then, with the help of Clotaire, massacres them.[20] In these cases, children were killed because they posed a threat as heirs.

During the second wave of invasions experienced by the West, in the ninth and tenth centuries, we find children being massacred again. Abbon of Saint-Germain describes the destruction orchestrated by the Normans at the end of the eleventh century:

> Children of all ages, young people, white-haired old timers, and fathers and sons and also mothers, they kill everyone. They massacre the husband before the eyes of his wife, the wife is the victim of slaughter; children perish in the presence of their fathers and mothers.[21]

When children were not killed in battle, they were sometimes taken prisoner and made into slaves.

Children as Slaves

Throughout the high Middle Ages, a proslavery economy persisted, as we can witness, for example, in the legislation of Visigothic Spain. Out of 498 legal texts issued on the Iberian Peninsula between the beginning of the fifth century and the beginning of the eighth century, 229 mention slavery. The great Visigothic landowners possessed hundreds of subjects, often children or adolescents who seem to have been particularly badly treated, victims of cruelty, mutilation, indeed even castration, a kind of human livestock subject to the whims of the master. Sometimes these children were slaves by birth since, as Isidore de Séville states, "According to the rules, the newborn assumes the condition of the lowest of its parents." Sometimes they were victims of raids and wars: Thuringians, Alamans, Bavarians, or Slavs captured by the Francs; Sueves enslaved by the Visigoths, Angles and Saxons sold in Italy by the Bretons; Irish, Flemish or Polish taken hostage during Viking raids; or captive Muslims remaining in Christian Mediterranean Europe following the *Reconquista**. Finally, they were sometimes sold by their own destitute parents or constrained by a legal decision. Some of the enslaved children went on to fulfill famous destinies. Bathilde (the future spouse of Clovis II), originally English, was sold as a slave at a very young age by Erchinoald, mayor of the palace of Neustrie a little before 650.

It would be wrong to believe that slavery came to an end with Christianity. The Church was perfectly adapted to the use of enslaved manpower. It is true that certain important ecclesiastical dignitaries sometimes became indignant over this practice and encouraged emancipation or recommended that captives be treated as human beings. It was at the end of the sixth century, after seeing English children sold as slaves to Rome by pagan merchants, that Pope Gregory the Great decided to send Augustine to convert the Angle peoples.[22] But, by relying on scriptural texts compiled in a time when slavery was a widespread reality, the clerics legitimized it by making it an institution of divine origin: men reduced to slavery attest to the condition of original sin and the baseness of humanity. More importantly, the end of support for slavery would have represented the undermining of an economic system entirely dominated by the ecclesiastical aristocracy. Christian ethics sometimes took second place to economic and political interests.

In his *Histoire des Lombard*, compiled at the very end of the eighth century, Paul Diacre relates an anecdote which tells us about children taken as slaves following battles but also about the resourcefulness required of small boys. In 610, after taking the city of Cividale, the Avars returned to their home and "decided to put the sword to all the Lombards already having reached maturity, and to draw lots for the captive women and children." Among them was Grimoald, the youngest son of Romilda, wife of the duke of Frioul Gisulf, who, after having tried to flee on horseback with his brothers, was captured by one of the Avars who had a faster horse. Seeing how young his prisoner was, the warrior "nevertheless judged him not worth the trouble of executing with a blow of the sword, and preferred to spare him in order to make him a slave. But the child,

> finely built, with sparkling eyes, and endowed with a bright mop of blond hair . . . full of grief at the idea of being dragged off as a captive in this way, *in his little soul roiling with grand designs*, drew from its sheath his little sword (the size he was able to carry at his age), and, with all his strength, struck the Avar who was carrying him on the top of the head. The blow went right to the brain, and the enemy was thrown from his horse. Then the little Grimoald turned back around on his mount, and fled, completely happy, and ended up joining his brothers again, causing them untold joy both by his deliverance and by the account he gave them of the death of the enemy.[23]

Reduced to extreme poverty, parents sometimes found themselves forced to sell their own children. At the beginning of the sixth century, Cassiodore relates how the peasants of southern Italy got rid of their children at the marketplace during a large fair:

> It is boys and girls who are put on display and categorized by age and sex; and if they are put up for sale, it is not a result of their captivity but of their freedom: their parents sell them, naturally, because they stand to profit by their servitude. And, in truth, they [the children] are, without a doubt, better off as slaves, if they are thus transferred from work in the fields to domestic work in the city.[24]

The chroniclers sometimes note that these sales, agreed upon by the children, can represent an improvement in their lot. In this type of society, as in our own, value judgments must not be made too quickly. As with abandonment, the sale of children did not always indicate a lack of affection. Jordanès tells how the Visigoths experienced a terrible famine when they first began to settle. Thus, they do not hesitate to sell their children, because they "want to assure the safety of their descendants: they can reconcile themselves more easily to seeing them lose their freedom than their lives, since a sold child will be fed miserably, but a kept child will surely die."[25]

By the same token, the "buyers" were not necessarily heartless masters. At the beginning of the eleventh century, near one of the gates of Barcelona, a rich Catalan landowner bought a young child upon whom she showered all her affection. We know that she showed herself to be particularly generous toward him in her will, bequeathing him great quantities of clothes and food, as if he were her son.[26]

It is difficult to know if selling children was very common and if it continued throughout the early Middle Ages. We know that the edict of Pistres (864) forbade fathers from making money from their children's servitude, except in the case of absolute destitution, and that, again in 1179, Canon 26 of the Third Latran Council condemned the practice of selling children to Saracens and to Jews.

FOUR

The Education of Children

The Meaning of Education

Contrary to what Philippe Ariès affirmed,[1] people of the high Middle Ages had not forgotten the meaning of education. They were always thinking hard about the different ways of transmitting their culture to the younger generation. About fifty terms were frequently used for expressing what was taught, instructed, or supervised.[2] This education had to begin as early as possible, because in the Middle Ages, people firmly believed that very young children possessed a sort of "unconscious memory," that everything children saw or heard at a young age marked them forever. They often compared the soul of the small child to clay or soft wax in which everything leaves an indelible mark. That was why parents and educators needed to be so careful about the words and gestures they used in addressing the very young.

Above all, teaching was supposed to take place through word and example (*verbo et exemplo*). Certainly, there is evidence of corporal punishment (much rarer at home than in monastic schools). We still have testimonies of pupils complaining of whippings. In 937, for example, to escape physical punishment, the students of Saint-Gall decided to set fire to the loft where the whips were kept. But those educators and recorders of monastic rules who recommended the use of corporal punishment always insisted upon the need for great moderation. As early as 540, Saint Benedict advises:

> The abbot must not allow children to be punished, or excommunicated, or whipped, because, even if one uses them for foolish or negligent monks, such strong measures can, on the contrary, make children worse than before, and not improve them.[3]

In the middle of the eighth century, Paul Diacre writes that "the master must act with moderation toward pupils and not whip them too much, because after the whip and punishment, they return very quickly to their misbehaving."[4] About 1025, Egbert de Liège also protests when

> Some stupid masters want their pupils to know what they have not learned; the mind is nourished from within, and the whip is of no assistance to it. . . . That unfortunate little one you shower with blows, he leaves as ill-formed as when he came.[5]

At the end of the eleventh century, a particularly severe and brutal abbot complains to Saint Anselm of the children being raised in the cloister. He reproaches them for being "corrupt and incorrigible" even though they are whipped day and night. Saint Anselm tries to prove to him that his methods are totally ineffective:

> It is because they do not feel from you any love, any pity, any kindness or gentleness, because they have no hope of seeing any good come from you, and they believe everything you do is provoked by hate and anger. And unfortunately, it will happen that as they grow up, hate and defiance will grow within them and they will be forever turned toward vice.[6]

All these thoughts on education, of course, come from clerics and a few aristocrats who were the only ones to leave us written records. But, for the very great majority of children in the early Middle Ages, knowledge of the culture or any kind of expertise was essentially learned within the context of the family. Only a minority were educated in schools and monasteries.

Children of the Common People

We know very little about the instruction of commoners' children in the high Middle Ages. No doubt they listened to sermons or to liturgical chants, and perhaps were instructed by images (statues, frescoes) which were already laden with pedagogical intent. In a good number of capitularies, Charlemagne insists that sermons incorporate knowledge of the *Credo* and the *Pater Noster*, as well as trinitarian dogma, summarizing the principal Christian precepts. We know, for example, that the *Capitula de presbyteris admonendis* of 809 required that all the laity, including children, be able to recite them. This minimum knowledge of religion no doubt expanded in the Carolingian period when translations of sacred texts into common languages became more widely available (earlier in the Germanic regions than in the Romanic) as well as *homéliares** to be used by the priests in charge.

In the very great majority of cases, peasant children had to be content with this kind of teaching, orally transmitted by the priest or by parents, because instruction in the letters was too expensive. The psalter, the book from which people learned to read, could not be bought by everyone, as this charming story recounted by Thomas de Cantimpré (mid-thirteenth century) shows:

> A young peasant begged her father to buy her a psalter so she could learn to read. "But how," he answered, "could I buy you a psalter, when I

can hardly earn enough to buy you bread each day?" The child was disappointed, but then she saw the Blessed Virgin appear to her in a dream, holding two psalters in her hands. Encouraged by this vision, she pleaded again. "My child," her father then said to her, "each Sunday, go find the school mistress of the parish; ask her to give you a few lessons, and try your best through your zeal to earn one of the psalters which you saw in the Virgin's hands." The little girl obeyed, and seeing her zeal, her companions at school got together to provide her with the book that she had so coveted.[7]

But Christian charity and solidarity had their limits, and the case of this little girl is exemplary because it is an exception. We know that, until at least the twelfth–thirteenth centuries, in rural areas of the West, the very great majority of men and women were illiterate. Children of commoners were put to work at a very young age, some in the family manse*, others on the estate reserve or in the manor workshop.

The lack of information available on the education of children among the common people in the high Middle Ages contrasts with the relative wealth of information concerning children in aristocratic circles. The ambitions that Charlemagne nurtured for his children provide a good summary of the ideal education for Carolingian princes:

> First of all, he wanted his children, the boys and the girls, to be introduced to the liberal arts, which he also applied himself to studying; then for his sons, when they were old enough, he had them learn to ride horseback, according to the Frankish custom, to use weapons, and to hunt; as for his daughters, to prevent them from becoming dull due to idleness, he had them practice working with wool as well as using the distaff and the spindle, and had them taught all those things which help to form them into honorable women.[8]

Religious Education

In the society of the high Middle Ages, as in our own, social inequality was blatant. Access to instruction was much easier for aristocratic children, and, as a result, their adherence to Christianity was stronger. They owned prayer books (often synopses of monastic services) and psalters. When, as children or adolescents, they left their parents' home to begin their own "adult" lives, often very young, nervous mothers, always concerned about their faith, would remind them of the essential virtues. We have three letters from the beginning of the seventh century addressed to Didier, the future bishop of Cahors, from his mother Herchenfreda. At the age of puberty, he had just left his parents' house to go to the court of King Clotaire II. Herchenfreda (the daughter of an aristocratic Gallo-Roman family from Albi) was worried about the dangers her son would face in a barbarian court. She exhorts him to think continually of God, to be chaste, charitable, and faithful to the king, to pay attention to his health and to let some-one know if he needs anything at court.[9]

But, without a doubt, the document richest in information on the aris-tocratic religious culture of the high Middle Ages is the famous *Manual* (*Liber Manualis*), of Dhuoda,[10] composed at Uzès between November 30, 841 and Feb-ruary 2, 843 by the wife of Bernard (whose father was the first cousin of Char-lemagne), the duke of Septimanie who defended the Carolingian empire against Muslim attacks. After the battle of Fontenay-en-Puisaye (June 22, 841), Bernard made peace with Charles le Chauve and decided to send his son Guillaume to him, asking him to pay him homage. Then, not long after the birth of his second son, Bernard asked Dhuoda to send him, too, to the king, so that he could see about his education. Thus, we have a mother deprived of her two sons, both in the same year. This is a large part of the reason why she decides to write this manual for Guillaume, fifteen years old, recommending that he later have it read to his brother. A *Liber manualis* is a little book (*liber*) which can be held in the hand (*manus*), and which is meant to be read daily: "You will find (in my book) a mir-ror in which you can contemplate the salvation of your soul."[11]

The originality of Dhuoda's *Manual* stems from the fact that it is not a theoretical treatise written by a cleric, but a work composed by a mother who wants most of all to address her own child. It allows us to assess the secular and religious culture of the laity in the middle of the ninth century. The work opens with this very moving statement:

> Aware that most women in this world have the pleasure of living with their children and seeing myself, Dhuoda, oh my son, Guillaume, separated and far away from you–and because of that, in such anguish and entirely filled with the desire to be helpful to you–I send you this small work, tran-scribed in my name, to read and to pattern yourself after. I would be happy if, in my absence, this book, by its presence, could remind you, when you are reading it, of what you must do out of love for me.[12]

She asks him, first of all, to be obedient to God, then to his father, then to King Charles. She insists especially on the respect that Guillaume owes to his father, since three chapters are devoted to this theme. Let us not forget that, at the time when she was writing this, the sons of Louis le Pieux were revolting against their father: "love, fear, cherish your father," she advises, "and remember that it is through him that you have attained your position in the world."[13]

So that Guillaume should be ever mindful of belonging to a great aristo-cratic family, Dhuoda likes to remind her son of his noble origins and the pres-tige of his ancestors, for whom she also asks him to pray. The faith in God that Dhuoda transmits to her son and which she calls him back to in this "mirror" rests primarily upon the fear of God. The Holy Spirit plays a larger part in it than Christ, Mary is almost absent, and the Eucharist almost never mentioned. For Dhuoda, spiritual sustenance comes from prayer and reading the sacred texts.

Thus she invites her son to pray many times during the day, to recite, like the monks, the canonical hours, and to read and meditate upon the Bible and the writings of the Church Fathers.

If the transmission of faith took place essentially through mothers,[14] the values of war and the military were taught by men.

Training in the Use of Arms

Physical training was just as fundamental for the young nobleman. That was how he prepared himself to assume the obligations that accompanied his birth. In the middle of the ninth century, the future count Géraud d'Aurillac "had been trained in secular exercises in his youth, as that was the rule for the children of nobility."[15]

The three pillars of military education were equitation, hunting, and the use of weapons. Thus, the young aristocrat was introduced to horseback riding very early and had to know how to use a bow, to release sparrow hawks and falcons for the hunt, and also to use the long sword, the javelin, the battle-ax, and the shield, for future battles. A young prince, about six years old, buried under the cathedral of Cologne in the sixth century, had in his tomb a long sword, a helmet, a shield, a battle-ax, a hook, a spear and some arrow tips.[16]

This training no doubt began very early. When, at the age of four, Louis le Pieux became king of Aquitaine, he was put on a horse, in arms, and led around his new realm. At eight years old, he was an excellent horseman.[17] Charles le Chauve was not yet four years old when, accompanying the adults on a hunting party and noticing a young doe:

> [He] longed to take off after her in pursuit, as his father always did, and he begged to be given a horse. He called passionately for weapons, a quiver, quick arrows, and wanted to follow her tracks, as his father did. He pleaded and pleaded. But his beautiful mother, warned him to keep his distance and refused his demands. If his tutor and his mother had not held him back, obstinate as children are, he would have taken off on foot. But the others, having gone off to pursue the young animal, captured it and brought it to the child. Then he seized weapons his size and struck the trembling creature. All the charm of childhood lingered about him.[18]

This example not only shows us the relative nature of the perception of "childhood charm," the child's strong desire at a very young age to imitate his father's feats, and the importance of maternal authority in tempering youthful ardor, but it also informs us that, with equipment adapted to his size, Charles le Chauve, hardly four years old, had already been initiated into the use of arms.

This purely physical training was complemented by moral instruction. In the area of war, as in his other activities, the young aristocrat had to learn the virtues which permitted weapons to be used with prudence and wisdom. Arnoul (born in 1161), son of Baudoin II of Guines, lord of Ardres, having just entered into adolescence, was very quickly recognized for his merits as first among the young men of Flemish nobility. Here are his noble qualities:

> He was nevertheless quick with weapons, inclined to virtue and integrity, known for his popularity at court, quick to render service, generous nearly to the point of extravagance. He had a cheerful face and a beauty surpassing all others his age at court; in addition to being gentle toward everyone, affable, and always gracious and proper in all things.[19]

We, of course, must allow for exaggeration in this perfect portrait, because the author (Lambert d'Ardres) was writing a work meant to please. It is most useful to read this text as an enumeration of the principle virtues a young aristocrat ought to possess.

Training in arms and the noble virtues necessary to retain one's rank was often the responsibility of a near relative. In Merovingian families, the *nutritores*, people in the same family (most often belonging to the maternal branch), were charged with "nurturing" royal or noble heirs. In the feudal Carolingian epoch, the practice of *commendatio*, which consisted of placing one's child with another family to be brought up was widely accepted. In order to complete their military education, groups of young men were frequently seen accompanying princes and kings. We know, for example, that Arnoul of Guines spent his childhood with his father and, when he acquired "the male vigor of adolescence," he often attended tournaments and found himself entrusted to "the venerated and memorable prince of Flanders, the count Philippe, to be instructed diligently and to be imbued with the customs and duties of knighthood."[20] In epic literature, a great number of nephews are brought up by their uncles. That is the case for Vivien, raised by Guillaume, and for Tristan, raised by Mark. This placement, especially if it occurred when the child was still young, created extremely strong bonds between the "nurturee" and his "adoptive father."

The transfer of children from one family to another could also be brought on by particular events. At the death of King Edwin of Northumbria in 633, his widow, Ethelbergha, "fearing the kings Eadbald and Oswald, sent her two children to Gaul to be raised in the court of King Dagobert, who was her friend."[21] Sometimes the dramatic circumstances of battle made it necessary for children to be educated far from their parent's home. Pemmo, the duke of Frioul, "gathered together the children of all the noblemen killed in battle . . . and raised them with his own, as if they were his own progeny."[22] When it was as brutal and involuntary as this, the transfer took place outside the sphere of kinship and children were moved about within a much wider radius.

When the young aristocrat was judged fit for combat, there was a ceremony for the presentation of arms, a ritual to integrate him into the ruling class:[23] Charlemagne waited for his son Louis to reach the age of thirteen before presenting him with the sword, and Louis le Pieux waited until his son Charles was fifteen years old. This was a matter of an absolutely essential ritual, a kind of rite of passage from childhood to adolescence. When it was not the father who presented the arms, it was another adult, sometimes the one who had seen to the youth's chivalric training, creating or reinforcing an alliance with the father of the child by means of this "adoption through arms."

The passage from childhood to adolescence was also marked by the cutting of the beard and hair. In the Merovingian period, princely children wore their hair long, a symbol of their power. Gundovald was "raised with diligent care, with curly locks of hair flowing down his back, as is the custom for their kings."[24] This head of hair was given special protection. The Salic law, for example, punishes whoever cuts the hair of a young boy without the consent of his parents by a fine of 45 sous of gold. It was often when the child came of age (twelve years) that his hair was cut (the Roman rite of *capillaturia*) or he was given his first shave (*barbatoria*).

The Aristocratic Daughter

Information concerning the life of young girls in aristocratic circles in the high Middle Ages is much less extensive than the information regarding boys. However, we know that, in general, they too received a very carefully planned education, learning to read, and even to write. Even in the sixth–seventh centuries, a period no doubt marked by a decline in education, many of them were literate. At the end of the seventh century, Fortunat writes of the young girls of the Aquitaine that they were as skilled with the pen as they were at weaving cloth.[25] This female education could take place within the context of the family or the palace but could be carried out as well, just as for boys, through spending a period of time at a monastery school.

We know that the daughters, especially, of the aristocracy married very young during the high Middle Ages. At the end of the sixth century, Vilithute was married at the age of thirteen and died in childbirth three years later.[26] Segolène, who became the abbess of Troclar in the area of Albi in the middle of the seventh century, was married at the age of twelve. Judith became the wife of the king of Wessex, Edilvulf I in October 856 when she was thirteen years old. Bathilde was about fifteen years old when the mayor of the palace of Neustrie, Erchinoald, married her to Clovis II in about 650–651 and was not yet seventeen years old when she gave birth to the future Clotaire III (born in 652). Hildegarde became the third wife of Charlemagne when she was hardly fifteen. Theophano, the Byzantine princess, was married to the emperor Othon II at the age of eleven (972). The mother of Guibert de Nogent had not yet reached twelve years old at the time of her marriage. These unions were all homogeneous: marriage took place within aristocratic circles. Gregory of Tours explains how his paternal great-uncle, Georges, of the senatorial class, looked for a daughter of a senator for his son, Gall (the future bishop of Clermont).

Among the peasantry, the facts are too limited to make comparisons, but the imbalance in the sex ratio in polyptychs from the beginning of the ninth century, which shows a relative under-representation of girls, could be explained by the fact that some of them had already left the family manse to work at the manor or to enter into marriage. The Church was very accommodating with regard to early marriage. Sometimes it even recommended it, explaining (Canon 9 of the Council of Pavie in 850) that by delaying the time of marriage for their daughters, parents took the risk of seeing them "corrupted," that is, of not being able to resist the temptation of losing their virginity.

Parish Schools and Episcopal Schools

Beginning from the sixth century, there were two types of schools to provide education outside of the familial and monastic contexts: parish and episcopal.

In Roman cities, ancient municipal schools remained in operation even up until the last part of the fifth century. Then, with Christianity, the parish schools appeared, whose function it was to train clerics (Arles or Bourges, for example). Canon 1 of the 529 Council of Vaison, asks that, to assure their succession, priests take charge of young students, instructing and preparing them by teaching them the psalter and the sacred texts. This decree is important because it constitutes the origin of presbyterial schools. These schools were opened to lay youths, since those who wished to leave school before entering the major orders could do so. The teaching body was composed solely of clerics, an original aspect of the medieval school. The young layman thus depended on the clergy for all instruction outside of the framework of the family.

The famous capitulary of Charlemagne dating from 789, entitled *Admonitio generalis* (general advice) includes a chapter entirely devoted to school: the priests are invited to teach children, serfs and free, reading, writing, arithmetic, and singing:

> Let the priests attract not only the children of those in servile conditions, but also the sons of free men. We want schools to be created to teach children to read. In all the monasteries and bishoprics, teach the Psalms, notation, singing, computation, grammar [that is, Latin]. . . . [27]

Beginning from the eleventh century, these schools multiplied, especially with the support given to them by merchants looking for elementary instruction (reading, writing, and arithmetic) for their sons so that they would be able to take over the family business.

Throughout, instruction took place in Latin. Thus, children became bilingual very quickly. They learned the twenty-four letters of the alphabet, and then began to make words. Learning to read began primarily with the psalter, but sometimes also involved the use of proverbs, sayings, or fables inherited directly from antiquity. At the same time as they learned to read, schoolboys and novices began to write with a bone or silver stylet on ivory or wood tablets covered with leather or wax, on bark, or parchment (rare and expensive). Then the schoolboy learned to count with the help of tokens or fingers. Teaching retained a playful quality, as this little math problem makes evident, presented in the form of a riddle attributed to Alcuin:

> Three young men each have one sister, the six travelers arrive at a river, but a single boat can only hold two people. Whereas morality requires that each sister cross with her brother. What are they going to do?[28]

Beginning from the tenth century, a new method of calculating was adopted, Arab in origin and then introduced into the Catalan schools: the abacus, a table for computing which allowed operations to be done very rapidly.

As for the episcopal schools, established in the bishops' quarters or in cloisters, they were directed by a specialized canon, the *scholasticus*. A child entered there at nine or ten years of age. He was tonsured, and remained at the school until he was about fifteen, at which time he had to choose between the lay life or taking the minor vows. Coeducation must have existed in episcopal schools, since certain statutes forbade it. It became established custom to reserve a portion of the chapter's goods for the masters as a form of remuneration. And masters could sometimes show themselves to be very severe, as does Odon of Tournai, at the beginning of the twelfth century:

> at the church he led his troop of nearly two hundred clerics in long lines as was his habit . . . not one who dared to speak to his neighbor, laugh, or mutter; not one who had the audacity to turn his eyes even a little to the right or left. . . .[29]

Over the course of the twelfth century, the regular canons tried to return to a more strict discipline. As a result, the episcopal schools received fewer and fewer children. We no longer find them mentioned, for example, in the statutes of the Prémontré and of Saint-Victor.

The canons of the Merovingian councils, and Carolingian capitularies especially, continually repeat that schools must be opened, proof, no doubt, of a lack of training and of negligence on the part of certain clerics. Théodulfe, bishop of Orléans, for example, demands again in 798:

> Let priests have schools in the agricultural areas and the large rural villages, and if the faithful want to entrust their small children to them to learn the letters, let them not refuse to receive them and teach them, and let them teach them with much love. . . . Let them demand no fee.[30]

In light of this last recommendation, we can surmise that if, in the Carolingian period, episcopal schools were common and dynamic, rural parish schools were no doubt quite rare.

Outsiders in the Monastery

It often happened that aristocratic families (and then, later, the families of merchants) entrusted their children to the monks for a period of time so that they could take charge of their education. Pépin, the son of Charles Martel, was placed into the monastery of Saint-Denis at a very young age. Sometimes contracts were drawn up between the abbot and the parents specifying the terms of admission, the receipt of goods (clothes, bedding), or the duration of the training.

In the lives of Irish saints, we come across cases of children a year or two old entrusted to cloisters and then later reinstated into male monasteries. But these examples are rare, and the great majority of documents show us instead that children were given over at about five or six years old, up to the age of ten or twelve. From the beginning of the Carolingian period with the expansion of Christianity, which sometimes led to massive numbers of aristocratic sons and daughters entering the monasteries, the monks, unnerved by these children who disrupted the meditative life, tried to take certain measures. In order to keep these schoolchildren separate from those preparing to take vows, the Council of Aix in 817 provided for an interior school meant to accommodate future monks, and an exterior school reserved for the laity. This measure was repeated many times afterwards, no doubt proving that it was not very effective. We know, however, that the monastery of Saint-Gall had this kind of double school. The plans of the religious establishment, drawn a bit after 817, locate the school for young laity on the north side of the church, separated from the rest of the monastery by a wall. Next to it, we find latrines, but no refectory or dormitory. To the east of the church is situated the monastic school, meant for the novices, who, on the other hand, have a refectory, dormitory and baths. In the eleventh century, in the spirit of Clunesian reform, this separation between *scolasticus exterior* and *scolasticus interior* could be found at Saint-Hubert and at Lobbes. Elsewhere, the two groups were no doubt mixed.

In the eleventh–twelfth centuries, the canonists continued to revolt against these young children who disrupted the monastic life. They reminded the monks that teaching was not their vocation and forbade the abbots to accommodate children destined for lay life. Nevertheless, in the twelfth century again, children filled the monasteries. We must remember that parents wishing to entrust their sons or daughters to the monks brought with them money and goods which enriched the convent. In the Germanic empire in the ninth–eleventh centuries, the monasteries took in mostly young aristocratic women, most often those ill-favored by nature or for whom the family had not provided a dowry. Their training there was both manual and intellectual. Some of them remained in cloisters, but others returned to the lay life. Duke Liudolf, for example, placed his five daughters in the abbey of Gandersheim. Three of them became abbesses, while the other two were married.

These abbeys (male or female) were not completely closed. Parents and friends could come to visit the children. Regulations required that these meetings transpire in a public place, however, sometimes through a screened window.

The attraction of the monastic life was sometimes so great that some children, placed there provisionally, wanted to remain apart from the world, contrary to their parent's plans for them. In the middle of the twelfth century, a merchant from Huy entrusted his son to the Cistercian monks of Viliers-en-Brabant, specifying that he wanted his son to learn reading, writing, and arithmetic, so that he would be able to take over his father's business. But the child was so happy in his monastic surroundings that he expressed the desire to stay there.[31] This example must certainly not be taken at face value. It is, of course, a matter of a hagiographical *topos* which aims at vaunting the superiority of the monastic over the worldly life. But the situation is no less plausible because of that.

The great majority of children entrusted permanently to monasteries, often at a very young age, were there against their will.

Oblation

Hildemar leaves us a commentary on the statutes of Saint Benedict (about 845),[32] which no doubt served as a manual in the monasteries of the ninth century. It informs us about the ritual of oblation (from the Latin, *offero*: to offer): when a child reached the age of six or seven years, the father (or, if the latter was deceased, the mother) came to give him over to the abbey, often with a certain sum of money or a piece of real estate. He approached the central altar with his son who held bread and water in his hands. There, before witnesses, he made a public vow to give him up. The child had to renounce his part of the inheritance which, according to Hildemar (but contrary to the dictates of the rule of Saint Benedict), had to be left to the monastery. It was very clearly a permanent renunciation of lay life. At the end of the eighth century, the young nobles offered to the abbey of Saint-Martin de Tours had to give up their horses and their arms, which were left at the saint's tomb, a ceremony meant to renounce the symbolic attributes of the aristocratic laity of the high Middle Ages.

Suger, Guibert de Nogent, Hugh of Lincoln, Orderic Vital, and the Venerable Bede were thus placed in monasteries as oblates. The last of these recounts:

> At the age of seven years, I was entrusted by my kin to the most reverend abbot Benoît (abbot of Wearmouth and Jarrow) for my education, and afterwards, to Céolfrid. Since then, I have passed my whole life within the walls of this monastery. . . .[33]

During the earliest medieval centuries, parental oblation was irrevocable, and the child, no matter what his vocation, had to remain at the monastery. To justify the permanent nature of the parental decision, legislators looked to Canon 49 of the Council of Toledo (633) which affirmed that there were two ways of becoming a monk: "be it by paternal engagement, be it by profession." In 726, in a letter addressed to Boniface, Pope Gregory II reminds him:

> You again add a question about whether those whose parents placed them within the walls of a monastery in their childhood to live there under its rule are permitted to leave at puberty and be married. We positively forbid this, because it is forbidden by God that those who have been offered to him by their parents see removed for them this obstacle to pleasure.[34]

But gradually, the idea developed according to which oblation had to be accepted by the child. Already in 817, Benedict required that the parental choice be ratified by the child himself. We know the famous case, from the beginning of the ninth century, of Gottschalk, the son of a Saxon count, offered to the abbot of Fulda at a very young age. At adolescence, claiming that he had not entered the monastery of his own free will, but under duress, he demanded his freedom. But Raban Maur, the new abbot at Fulda, refused to "liberate" him, and wrote his famous *On the Oblation of Children*[35] in which he reaffirms that the engagement of the parents is irrevocable. Finally, by imperial decision, Gottschalk was forced to remain a monk and sent to the monastery of Orbais, near Soissons.

Even if the Council of Worms (868) still defended irrevocable oblation, the Gottschalk affair, no doubt not an isolated case, reveals a change in behavior with regard to oblation. The new orders, such as Cluny, Cîteaux, the Chartreux, or the Templiers, did not accept the oblation of children, less because the institutions themselves rejected them than because the presence of children seemed to them to disrupt the smooth functioning of monastic life. Thus, the number of oblates decreased very rapidly beginning from the twelfth century. In 1194, Celestine III officially authorized an oblate to terminate his parents' act of engagement when he reached puberty, and then, in the middle of the fifteenth century, Martin V permanently banned oblation.

Monastery Life

Monastic rules and custom, as well as treatises written for the training of novices supply us with precise information on the daily life of young monks. We know that great attention was given to their upbringing. Udalrich, for example, writes:

> When I saw with what zeal the children were supervised day and night, I said to myself that it would have been very difficult for even the son of a king to be raised with more care in his father's palace than the least of the children at Cluny.[36]

This supervision (*custodia infantum*) seems exemplary, the dream of all modern-day teachers, since three or four masters (*magistri*) were designated to look after ten children. Above all, education was based on constant control over the children and especially over the adolescents awakening to sexuality. According to Hildemar in the middle of the ninth century, if masters were obliged to take recourse in physical punishment, it was precisely because their supervision had not been adequate.

In the abbey, life was divided up according to the monastic offices of the day, which the children had to attend. They rose very early (no doubt at about two or three in the morning) to recite the nocturnal office and matins*. Then they went to the monastery school where, seated on stools around the master's pulpit, they read and chanted verses that they learned. When they knew their psalms by heart, they had to recite a section of them before the abbot. The *Rule of the Master*, from the beginning of the sixth century, fixed at three the number of hours of daily teaching. Monastic customs forbade children from speaking or making any signs during lessons. Teaching methods differed hardly at all from those employed by the parish or episcopal schools we have described. Then, after another office (sexte), they went in silence to the refectory where they were carefully supervised. They had to always be accompanied by a monk when they went out, even to the latrines. After compline* (about six o'clock), always maintaining silence, the novices returned to their dormitory, separate from the one for the monks.

Hard days, certainly, but often tempered by moments of relaxation and play. Actually, the master sometimes took the children to a meadow or some such place where they could relax. Times for recreation were arranged for them, for horseback riding, swimming, playing with batons or hoops, and gardening. During the important liturgical holidays, they were granted a few days of vacation. Moreover, children were not required to respect all the fasts, especially if they were considered too weak to endure them. They were permitted to eat more often than the adults (three or four times a day), but in smaller quantities, and they were still sometimes given meat, unlike their elders. When they were sick, they were given very special attention in the infirmary. They were sometimes allowed to go back to bed if they had a difficult time staying awake between matins and lauds*.

Also, they sometimes played practical jokes on the monks, as an *exemplum* of Etienne de Bourbon, from the middle of the thirteenth century, reports:

> In a certain priory, whose name I do not wish to mention, lived some very unenlightened monks, who, after spending the night drinking, eating, and gossiping, found themselves very tired when the bells rang for matins. They got up nevertheless, half asleep, and tried to begin the office. But, as they could not keep themselves awake and their heads kept falling into their books at every verse, they ordered the children in the choir to chant along with them. After a few minutes, all the monks had fallen asleep again. Then one of the children, who had been waiting for this moment, signaled to his companions to be quiet. At first, they all kept very still; then, seeing that nobody was moving, they began to play as they pleased. After they had been amusing themselves for quite a while, one of them suddenly made a lot of noise and cried out in a loud voice: *Bendicamus Domino*. Immediately, the monks, waking up with a start, responded in chorus together: *Deo gratia!*
>
> Each of them remained convinced that the others had said matins with the choir children and that the office was completed, and they hurried right back to their beds. And that is how the devil, with the help of sleepiness, his accomplice, destroys all the fruitfulness of prayer.[37]

Girls in the Cloister

It is always more difficult to find information on the young girls who entered the monasteries. Sometimes, monastic regulations specified that given rules applied equally to the females, or mentioned specific aspects of the girls' cloistered life.

We know that aristocratic Frankish families nearly always counted on one or more daughters entering the monastery. They were also received there beginning at six or seven years old. Whether they remained for a period of time or permanently, the education that they received was practically the same as what was offered in aristocratic homes, that is, sewing, embroidery and reading, sometimes writing. Some girls even redid their rooms in the school, which was not looked upon favorably at all. We know that they also had to learn the psalter by heart, as the set of rules used by the sister of Césaire d'Arles, Césarie (early sixth century) indicates, or the one in effect at the female monastery of Sainte-Croix of Poitiers, founded about 560 by Radegonde, the wife of the Merovingian king, Clotaire I.

The rules of Waldebert of Luxeuil, from the beginning of the seventh century, supply us with the most ample information:

> they must be brought up with piety and affection, but also with discipline, so that, at this tender age, they will not be stained, no matter how slightly, by the vice of laziness and thoughtlessness, and so that, later, they can be corrected of it. Thus it is necessary to supervise the children with much care, so that they never go here or there without older girls, and always, controlled by their discipline, and instructed in the fear of God and in the love of the good doctrine, they seek out the religious life. Let them acquire the habit of reading so that they learn at a young age what they must do later. In the refectory, let their tables be placed next to those of the older girls; two or more among the older ones who possess religious zeal must take their places beside the children, and keep watch attentively over their education. It is the abbess who decides the hours for meals and for sleeping. Let it be fully noted who is the guardian of virtues.[38]

Thus, despite appreciable differences according to the social level, in the high Middle Ages, girls and boys were raised, educated, and trained with care. Beginning from the eleventh and twelfth centuries, economic and social conditions clearly improved, and the sources of available information allowing us to elaborate upon the history of the child multiply. In particular, and to a much greater degree than for the centuries preceding, they allow us to observe the child within the family.

FIVE

The Child within the Family

The Family, Immediate or Extended?

For a long time, historians opposed the "large patriarchal family" of the high Middle Ages (uniting under one roof collaterals, ascendants, and descendants) to the "conjugal family" (grouping together the father, mother, and unmarried children) of the centuries that followed. This evolutionist idea of the history of the family is now being called into question: there is just as much evidence for the nuclear family in the earliest medieval centuries. For example, a study of a list of slaves from the ninth century, coming from the cartulary of Farfa in central Italy, shows the very clear predominance of the conjugal family, since 65 percent of the households are composed of a couple with or without children.[1] Out of some 600 Catalonian contracts of sale from about the year 1000, nearly 90 percent concern only conjugal groups (father, mother, children), infra-conjugal groups (widows with children) or single people.[2] In the Merovingian and Carolingian periods, the manse is concrete proof of the existence of the nuclear family, since its acreage was supposed to be sufficient to support this family unit, whether in France, Italy, or England.

But this much is certain: in the twelfth and thirteenth centuries, the immediate family appears at the center of familial relationships even more clearly than before. Archaeology shows us that the size of dwellings shrank; houses were subdivided, either on the ground floor or by building a second story. In Picardie, for example, after 1175, the number of deeds contracted by large familial groups decreased, to be replaced by those contracted by couples.[3] It is, of course, necessary to be prudent here, because regional differences are very great with regard to the size of families, but the trend seems fairly general. Increasingly abundant narrative sources often involve the nuclear family and parent-child relationships.

Families, Biological and Blended

The phenomena of "broken" and "reconstructed" families, which so preoccupy sociologists at the end of the twentieth century, are not new. If today, divorce is the main reason for the family unit breaking up, in the very great majority of cases in the Middle Ages, it was the result of the death of a parent. Indeed, judging from the demographic situation of the Ancient Regime,[4] a period close enough in time to warrant comparison, we can estimate that 30–40 percent of children did not live their entire childhood with both their natural parents. In other words, more than a third of all children lived in reconstructed families. This "circulation" of children in the Middle Ages was reinforced by placement in foster homes, with nurses, or in apprenticeships, by couples separating, and by abandonment. It is common to come across children in narratives who live with relatives who are not their natural parents: nephews or nieces placed there after a parent died, or transferred from a large family to one lacking heirs, children placed with nurses, etc.[5] *Coutumiers*, collections of the customs of a province or a country, always devote several chapters to the right of leasing out or of keeping children, a legal preoccupation which no doubt attests to a widespread phenomenon.

Maternal Love

Contrary to what Philippe Ariès is believed to have shown,[6] the feelings that the medieval mother had for her child were very strong. A great many documents attest to her affection and tenderness. A good example from the very beginning of the fourteenth century is offered by this Catharist woman of Montaillou whom the inquisitors had condemned for heresy. She had to leave her home knowing that she would never again see her infant (she died at the stake); this is how the narrator describes to us the scene of their separation:

> She wanted to see him before going away; seeing him, she embraced him; then the child began to laugh; as she had just begun to leave the room where he was lying, she returned to him again; again the child began to laugh; and so it went, many times over. So it was that she could not bring herself to part with the child.[7]

A moving and terrible scene which says much about the emotions felt by the mother for her child. In *L'Escoufle*. by Jean Renart, a novel written at the beginning of the thirteenth century, another mother must also part with her child of three years, whose father is asking for him, a temporary separation, but just as difficult to bear:

> But I love him more than anything, she said, there is nothing more beautiful than him. As long as I am looking at him, I can feel no irritation, or anger, or boredom. He is my hope, my joy, my precious gem and my pleasure.[8]

After which, she reaches out her arms and the child rushes to her. And, so as to enjoy one last time the joys of maternal love before the cruel departure, she lays him down to sleep in her own bed. In the morning, against her will, she has to place him on a horse, taking care to prop him up with a big cushion and bursting into sobs at the moment of parting. At the beginning of the twelfth century, Guibert de Nogent recounts a mother's anger when she discovers that her son has been severely beaten by the master to whom she has entrusted him to make him into a cleric:

> One day, in class, I had been beaten: the class which was nothing other than a certain room in our house. . . . I had come running to my mother, after having been seriously beaten, certainly more than I had deserved. She began asking me, as was her habit, if I had been hit that day; and, so as not to appear to be denouncing my tutor, I categorically denied it. Then, despite what I said, she lifted up my clothes (what one calls a tunic, or perhaps a chemise), and she began to examine my little arms, marked with bruises, and the skin of my poor back a bit swollen all over from the blows of the rod. Crying out loudly at the sight of this cruelty inflicted at my tender age, upset, agitated, her eyes full of tears of sadness, she said to me, "Since this is how it is, you will never become a cleric: you will no longer have to undergo punishment in order to learn Latin!"[9]

But Guibert de Nogent's desire to become a cleric is so strong that he succeeds in convincing his mother to let him continue studying with this cruel master.

In the accounts of miracles from the twelfth and thirteenth centuries, the mother keeps her small child under strict supervision, always showing him the utmost attention. When she goes out to church or to the fields, she brings her baby with her or leaves him with a relative. If, by some misfortune, an accident takes place, her pathetic reaction conveys her distress. She screams at the sight of the wounded body or the corpse of her child, pulls out her hair, claws at her face. Not just figures of rhetoric, these grief-stricken reactions convey undeniable maternal attachment. After the emotional shock subsides, she tries to win favors from the saint (or from the Virgin) through promises and prayers, hoping they will intercede before God. Thus she spends whole days in the sanctuary in prayer. At the moment of the miracle, she bursts with joy. Her sincere and poignant thanks addressed to the saint or to God also convey the strength of feeling of medieval mothers for their children. In the middle of the twelfth century, in England, a child hardly three years old

> suddenly stricken with disease, let out appalling cries and was as desperately exhausted as his parents. One of them said to the other, "Take the child, warm him in your arms." She obeyed and cuddled him, humming softly, as she always did, but neither the kisses nor caresses of his mother made him feel any better. Very gently, she put him back into his cradle again, but even then, the pain did not let up.[10]

The child dies, but thanks to the prayers and invocations of his parents, which prompt the saint's intervention, he comes back to life.

In the statutes of a women's monastic order from early thirteenth-century England, the sixth comfort of God is compared to the joys derived from the game of hide-and-seek between a mother and her child:

> She parts with him and hides and leaves him alone. He looks for her everywhere, calling, "Mama! Mama!" and crying a little. Then, with outstretched arms, she rushes toward him, takes him up, and pulls him close to embrace him and dry his tears.

The author explains that God can sometimes abandon a nun, just as this mother does, and she is then obliged to "call and cry for him like the little baby does for his mother," until He finally consoles her in her distress.[11] This metaphor which associates God or the Church to the mother, and the believer to a small child recurs throughout Christian mythology. In the thirteenth century, Guillaume Durand compiles all the names given to the Church: "Sometimes it is called by the name of Mother, because each day, through baptism, it delivers to God his spiritual sons."[12] In the iconography from the end of the Middle Ages, it is not unusual to see the Church represented by the allegorical figure of a mother teaching her children.

Maternal love is often presented and judged as more excessive, more unrestrained, more instinctual, and more visceral than that of the father. When a child falls ill, has an accident, or dies, authors show its mother transformed by a "maternal solicitude" or "driven by her maternal depths," or again, "returned to the pains of childbirth." Now, in the Middle Ages, excess, the absence of moderation, is always condemned. Philippe de Novare, for example, writes: "One must not show one's child too much love, because he becomes boastful and takes of the habit of wrongdoing."[13] This way of presenting maternal feelings no doubt conveys the actual situation as much as it does the clerical perception and representation of women in their maternal role.

"Cruel Mothers": The Saint and the Stepmother

In medieval sources, there are two kinds of women who are bad mothers, "cruel mothers": the saint and the stepmother. But, they exist, through the pen of the clerics, for essentially ideological reasons.

Women saints, for whom certain biographers have left us *vita*, nearly always experience anti-maternal feelings. At the end of the thirteenth century, Marguerite de Cortone abandons her illegitimate son "without a single maternal qualm" when she enters the Franciscan Tiers-Ordre to dedicate her life to the poor and to Christ.[14] Angèle de Foligno, a contemporary of Marguerite, a visionary and mystic, thanks God for having made her mother, her husband, and her children die, because these successive deaths permit her to consecrate herself entirely to religion.[15] This stereotypical attitude is supposed to show the extent to which one can dedicate oneself to God and give up worldly joys.

Besides the saint, the other medieval bad mother is the stepmother, that is, the second wife of the father. Here we find ourselves confronted with a grave contradiction: in all the sources, this woman is the archetype of the cruel mother, and yet, she represents an everyday reality, since the death of the mother and the father's remarriage are common events. In the Middle Ages, as today, the term, stepmother, is pejorative. In the middle of the twelfth century, wanting to demonstrate how roughly nature treats man beginning from the time of birth, Guillaume de Saint-Theirry writes:

> While nature, the good mother, protects other living beings, for man, she changes into a sorry stepmother, she throws him to the ground to make him immediately cry and wail, while no other animal knows tears. . . .[16]

From the beginning of the Middle Ages, the stepmother is always a figure of great cruelty. Gregory of Tours, for example, mentions the second wife of the king of the Burgondes, Sigismond, who showed herself to be very severe with Sigéric, the son of his first marriage. She "comes very quickly," he writes, "to detest this son and to lose her temper with him, as is the habit of stepmothers," and she urges her husband to have the child strangled.[17] In the *exempla* or later accounts of miracles, we find this same image of the second mother. Here is just one example out of many showing the way in which clerics portray her: a man remarries following the death of his wife, by whom he has had a child. After many years of life together, no descendant is produced by this second marriage:

> [the wife] ate her heart out with the venom of envy; and, armed with the hatred a stepmother bears toward her stepson, she wanted to make him pay the penalty for her infertility, which was not his fault. And one day, as was her custom, she gave him bread for his meal, to which she had secretly added poison. The child ate it. The poison spread rapidly, first reaching the spiritual organs and then the digestive one. Infected, his body began to swell up, and he was completely deprived of the use of his corporal senses.[18]

All the ideological ingredients are assembled here to make this woman the stereotype of the bad mother. The son is an only child. It is through him, and him alone, that the paternal patrimony can be transmitted to assure the continuation of the line. The crime becomes still more abominable. The stepmother is jealous and does not accept her infertility. Not being able to procreate herself, that is, to give the couple another heir, she seeks her revenge on the son of the first marriage. Not being the child's biological mother, her role should be that of a nurturing foster mother. Whereas, appropriately enough, it is through food that she kills the child by secretly poisoning him.

When such accounts are not centered on this theme toward some edifying end, fortunately, we sometimes do see better relationships established between the second mother and her child.

How then to explain this fury, this hatred against the stepmother? It is clear that this is a matter of an image which dates back to pre-Christian times, and which builds upon an ancient anthropological foundation. Many stories (such as Cinderella) develop this theme. The stepmother is also condemned because she corrupts the blood of the new family. In French legal documents from the thirteenth century, the "cruel mother" is the one who comes to drain the inheritance, who represents a threat because, in general, she is much younger than the husband, and, consequently, she will most probably die after he does. Thus, she transfers the paternal inheritance to another family. For aristocratic families, the second mother threatens the family blood and fortune. But, beyond this anthropological basis, a specifically Christian explanation also exists. The medieval Church remains deeply opposed to remarriage. That is why those who do not remarry are more highly regarded. In medieval sources, the widow's image is the exact opposite of the stepmother's.

Paternal Tenderness

If paternal love seems, on the whole, more measured than that of the mother, it remains no less strong, and there are many medieval examples demonstrating the existence of the sensitive father, close to his children, sharing their joys and sorrows. In the fabliau, *Celui qui bota la pierre* [The one who kicked the stone], written at the beginning of the fourteenth century, a peasant returns from his work. Here is how the reunion that evening with his son unfolds:

> When the child saw his father arriving, he rushed over to greet him. He met him at the doorstep, jumped about happily, and threw himself upon him, saying, "Lovely father, God keep you and give you joy and bring you honor." The man embraced his child and happily picked him up.[19]

In the accounts of miracles, there are many fathers who suffer and shed abundant tears over the sickness or death of their child, rush off to the doctor's, run from sanctuary to sanctuary (sometimes covering dozens of kilometers) begging for divine intervention which will allow the child to become well again or come back to life. There are also many who remain at the tomb of some saint for days and days with their sick son or daughter, pleading and praying, and many who burst with joy when a miracle saves their child.

Unfortunately, not all fathers benefit from the effects of divine intervention and, powerless and beaten, must witness the death of their child. Let us observe the grief of Filippo De Bernardo Manetti, of Florence, who, during the plague of 1449–1450, in the space of a month and a half, loses his wife, seven of his daughters, and his only son, fourteen and a half years old. Here is the eulogy that he writes for him, in his "book of reason" (*ricordanza*): "I don't believe that many are born who compare to him, none more obedient, more respectful, more pure or more prudent, or more appreciated by all who cast eyes on him." This Italian father especially admires the way in which his son, a good Christian, prepared himself for death:

> When he reached the end, this was an admirable thing to see, at this still green and fresh age of fourteen and a half, aware that he was going to

die. . . . Three times he confessed during his illness with great diligence, and then received the body of Our Lord Jesus Christ with so much contrition and reverence that those watching were filled with devotion; finally, having requested the holy oil and continuing to chant with the clerics surrounding him, he patiently rendered his soul to God.[20]

Let us listen to another Florentine, Giovanni Morelli, and to his long and terrible suffering over the death of his oldest son, Alberto, nine years old, in June 1406. To carry out his "work of grieving," because unbearable pain must be spoken or written down, this father notes with extreme precision the final events and actions in the life of his son, from May 19, the date on which Alberto falls ill, until June 5, the date he dies. He relates the mortal agony which, powerless, he must witness. His son no longer eats, no longer sleeps, suffers terribly. This testimony is all the more poignant because the father who is writing it lost his own father when he was two years old, and his mother, quickly remarried, did not raise him. Giovanni thinks about being able to be for his son the father whom he hardly knew, and here is death cutting short his fatherhood just as, earlier, it took away his father and brought his childhood to an abrupt end. This death is going to haunt him even more because, when his son gives up his soul, many relatives and friends gather in his chamber, but, until the end, no priest is present. Unlike his fellow citizen, Filippo Di Bernardo Manetti, here is a father who cannot stop mourning his son, because he did not receive last rites. He has not secured for his son a "good death." The whole family leaves the house for one month. For six months, Giovanni does not enter the child's bed chamber. He writes:

> His image is always before our eyes, we recall his footsteps, his way of being, his words and his actions, night and day, at lunch and at dinner, inside as well as outside. . . . We think that he has seized a knife to strike us at the heart.[21]

It is only on the anniversary of Alberto's death that Giovanni is freed of his remorse, because his son appears to him in a dream and reassures him that thanks to his prayers, he is saved.

Filial Love

Signs of filial love are much less abundant than signs of parental affection. They often come from adults remembering nostalgically the affection they felt for their parents, especially for their mother. We know of the very beautiful passages from the twelfth century that Guibert de Nogent devoted to his mother:

> Thanks be given to you, my God, to you who instilled my mother with such virtue and beauty! Indeed, the earnestness of her bearing was enough to awaken my contempt of all vanity. . . . Almighty God, you inspired in her from earliest youth, you know, the fear of your name as well as a reso-

lute spirit to resist all impulses. Let us remark how rarely it occurs, how nowhere does one find among women of high standing a reticence like hers, a result of your grace, combined with so great a repugnance for denigrating those who lack it.[22]

Another cleric gives us a moving confession during the public funeral oration which he addresses to his mother on the day she dies. This comes from Frédéric de Hallum (who died in 1175), parish priest of Frise, then a Prémontré canon:

> I am shattered by the departure of my mother—no one will reproach me for this . . . I do not forget her kindnesses, especially those that she lavished upon me from the midst of her poverty during my scholarly exile, so that I should not falter in the study of God. Oh how many times she zealously gave food, warmth, and aid to the poor, asking them to pray to God for my salvation. . . . I owe so much to her . . . . That is the reason for my tears, my sighs, this sorrow that I feel. That is why my words are full of sadness. . . .[23]

If these testimonies come from adults, it is, of course, because in the Middle Ages, children (and the young in general) did not leave writings revealing their feelings with regard to their parents while they were still dependent upon them, living in the family home. But it is also because educators considered filial love to be a less strong emotion than what parents bore for their children. Giles of Rome, an Aristotelian thinker of the thirteenth century, writes:

> Fathers and mothers love their children more intensely than the children do them, because the love of fathers and mothers for their children lasts longer than the love of children for them, and because when they are born, they don't have enough judgment to allow them to recognize their parents and thus they love them by nature . . . fathers and mothers are more sure of their children . . . the children can only be assured by a few signs or by hearsay or because they see that one person has greater confidence in them than the others. Because at their birth, children cannot know which mother bore them or which father engendered them. . . . Because the more certain love is, the stronger it is.[24]

Consequently, for Giles of Rome, if filial love is less strong than parental love, the reason is because it is not founded upon the certitude that there is a genetic link between father, mother, and child.

As children grew up, a generational conflict sometimes developed, especially at the time of adolescence, which often represented, historically just as today, a time of very great tension between parent and child. When they were old, parents had no financial security to guarantee their survival. If they had already passed on their inheritance to their children, the latter's ingratitude could prove to be dramatic. We know the famous fabliau of the *Housse Partie* (The Divided Cover): a rich merchant who wants to secure the marriage of his only son to the daughter of a noble knight without a fortune agrees to relinquish all his possessions to his son. The son, in return, promises to take care of his father until his death. As the years pass, the couple (especially the wife) have less and less patience for the old man, who is quickly perceived as a useless mouth to feed. Thus, a decision is made to turn him out. Before leaving the house, the old man asks his son at least to give him a blanket to protect him from the cold. The son consents, in order to be sure of getting rid of his father. He then asks his ten-year-old son to go to the stable and bring back a horse blanket and give it to his grandfather. The child, "who is full of good sense," brings a blanket, takes his knife, and cuts it in two. He gives half of it to his grandfather, and, to his father's astonishment, he explains that he is keeping the other part for him when he is old. The father then understands his son's lesson, and decides to keep taking care of his father as he had originally promised.[25]

Religious Education Provided by Mothers

The mother played a fundamental part in her children's lives, no matter what their age. It was she who provided their basic education, when they were children certainly,[26] but also when they were older. The transmission of the Christian faith was essentially carried out within the family, taking an oral form, and the mother playing the primary role.[27] Jean de Joinville writes, for example, concerning Saint Louis: "God looked after him through the good teachings of this mother who taught him to believe in God and to love him." We know, in fact, that Blanche de Castille was particularly attentive to his intellectual and religious education, having him listen to sermons at a very young age. A perfect example which appears in all the sources: during her trial, Joan of Arc declares that it was her mother who taught her the three prayers that all good Christians must know: the *Pater Noster*, the *Credo* and the *Ave Maria*.

The mother took the children to church, showed them the sacred images and statues, taught them the gestures for the prayers. This religious teaching by the mother no doubt involved all the objects of everyday life. We find alphabet bowls decorated with crosses, rosary beads, abacuses, and religious toys for children dating from the end of the Middle Ages, which show that this instruction in Christian values often involved play.

Medieval mothers played a particularly important role in the education of daughters, transmitting to them certain qualities, certain know-how in domestic matters and matters of love in order to prepare her for her future life as a wife. Fabliaux like to exploit this complicity between the mother and the adolescent, this shared cunning which, according to the clerics writing these accounts, was used to trick men. The development of this theme in literature shows the uneasiness that men and the Church felt watching values being passed from mother to daughter, those "secrets of good women" which eluded them.

The "New Fathers"

On this topic, we must put an end to an accepted idea: up until he was seven years old, the child (especially boys) was supposed to have lived in a world of women, and suddenly, he supposedly left this den of females to be forced out into a world of men and to learn a trade. Using a little common sense, is it possible to imagine, especially among medieval peasantry (that is, nearly the entire population) who often lived in a single room, a situation like this, in which the father is distant, even absent for all the early years of his child's life? In fact, many sources show fathers at their children's sides, male or female, from their first years on. In the accounts of miracles from the twelfth and thirteenth centuries, the father's presence, from at least the child's third year on, is as pronounced as the mother's, and we often witness him being "motherly."[28] At the end of the twelfth century, for example, a Flemish father leaves to repair his boat with his companions and, because his wife is pregnant, he brings his little two-year-old daughter with him.[29] A century later, in Saint-Denis, we find a father by the side of the little Marote, three and a half years old, playing in the courtyard of the house, another father holding his little girl of one and a half years under the arms, teaching her to walk, and a third father who, when his children suffer from ague, takes their temperatures everyday at the same time, from the month of August until Easter, that is, for eight months.[30] When a couple had many children, or when the mother was disabled, clearly, the father had to take care of all their children. At the end of the thirteenth century, in Saint-Denis, a certain Robert Rossel, husband of a blind woman, bathed and fed his very young children.[31] After a woman gave birth, while waiting for the churching rituals,* the father surely took over the day-to-day care of the youngest children in most homes, because poor peasants did not have servants to stand in for confined mothers.

But sometimes it was because of maternal inadequacies that fathers had to provide their infants with love and protection. In 1424, the young wife of Jean Lambert, a Parisian silversmith living at the Notre-Dame bridge, gave birth to their third child, whom she was not able to nurse as she had the first two. The father then sees to placing him with a nurse at Crosnes, near Villeneuve-Saint-Georges. But, learning that he is not in good health, the father decides to bring him back home along with his wet-nurse. A serious depressive, the mother tries to commit suicide several times. This "nurturing father," with a wife who can no longer assume her role as mother, takes complete charge of his little son's life, whose health remains unstable. He has him taken on a pilgrimage to Saint-Germain-des-Prés to improve his condition. Finally, Jean Lambert is not able to prevent tragedy: the mother drowns her three-month-old baby by throwing him into a well at the house of her father who lives near Saint-Merry.[32]

Thus, in the Middle Ages, fathers assumed those functions which today would be considered as belonging to the "new fathers." In iconographic sources, paternal and maternal roles are often just as interchangeable with regard to the nursery. In images portraying a father, the scriptural model of Joseph asserts itself. In Nativity scenes, there is a double image of Jesus' foster father: on the one hand, a jealous, sullen individual, seemingly indifferent to the Virgin and the Child, appears in a corner of the picture somewhere; these are the most well-known representations. On the other hand, an attentive father who goes to look for wood for a fire, pours bath water, mends the bellows, gets the fire up "on all four feet" by blowing on the coals, supplies the baby cereal, does the washing, dries his son's blankets by one corner of the fire, shakes the rattle, rocks the infant in his arms, and then, when Jesus is a little bigger, plays spin the top with him or repairs his toys. This last group of images is less well known, obscured by historians of the nineteenth and early twentieth centuries, disinclined to show this vision of the father, who would no doubt disturb bourgeois notions of the family.

The most secular images of the late Middle Ages let us witness great complicity between father and child, in work as well as play: little ones gather acorns as the father cuts down an oak, scare up birds in the fields while he sows wheat, hold the sheep's feet while he shears them, and, during the grape harvest, want to help trample the grapes in the vat.

As a result, in literary sources as well as iconographical documents, even before the famous advice of Jean Gerson who, at the beginning of the fifteenth century, writes: "let us not be ashamed of speaking to children as good and kind mothers would," fathers "mothered." The development of the worship of Saint Joseph, beginning in the fourteenth century, was, no doubt, only the result and most visible expression of the existence of a nurturing and tender father in the Middle Ages. Saint Joseph was honored because he remained chaste in his married life and he was not the natural father of Jesus. He was the symbol of the father who, outside of all ties of carnal filiation, defended his wife and child out of his love for God.

As the child grew up, the father's role as educator remained just as important. Pedagogues advised fathers to "chasten" their children, that is, to reprimand and instruct them. This word does not necessarily imply corporal punishment. Even if some tracts advocate physical punishment, many of them only recommend using it as a last resort, when persuasion has failed, and insist upon the need for great moderation when applying the rod in order for it to be effective. In the narrative sources, we rarely find children being struck by their fathers. The few cases of child beating nearly always involve orphans. The father in these kinds of narratives protects his children, but does not beat them.

Just as with monks and novices in monasteries, fathers had to teach their children *pro verbo et exemplo*. With words and gestures which sometimes left such deep impressions in children's minds that they remembered them clearly as adults. This was the case with Jean Gerson (1363–1429) who recalls his father, standing against the wall of the house, arms stretched out at his sides, solemnly saying to him, "Look here, my son, this is how your God was crucified, and how he died, for your salvation."[33]

If medieval paternal education takes place with more gentleness than violence, it remains no less of a necessity. The absence of paternal guidance has a dramatic effect on the rest of one's life: a very famous *exemplum*, often repeated in educational tracts, tells the story of a badly brought up child committing small thefts under the amused gaze of his father who thinks that this evil tendency will pass with maturity. However, he is wrong. The child grows up and commits more and more serious crimes, so many and so serious that he ends up being tried and condemned to hanging. As he is being led to the gallows, he pleads with his guards to let his father come to him to embrace him. Hearing this perfectly natural filial desire, the hangmen take pity on him and authorize his father to come, one last time, to embrace his child. The son then leans toward his father, as if to embrace him, and rips off his nose. Upon which follows a moral aimed at denouncing too lenient fathers. In the same vein, several fabliaux (*Estula, De Barat et de Haimet, Des trois larrons*) focus upon the theme of the two thieving brothers in order to show the deficiencies and social disorder represented by the lack of paternal education. Their vice is always explained by bad or non-existent parental guidance.

Girls and Boys

Indisputably, parents wanted boys more than girls. Medical or paramedical literature (often stemming from a mix of scientific knowledge and popular beliefs), which gives formulas for predicting a child's sex or conceiving a boy or a girl, tend to favor the male child. It is thought, for example, that a woman carrying a boy always has better color and is happier whereas a woman pregnant with a girl is pale and seems to be in poor health. The left-right opposition recurs as well in these types of beliefs. If the belly extends out further to the right or if the right breast is larger than the left (the unlucky side), it is a boy. These beliefs rest on the fact that in the Middle Ages, referring back to Hippocrates, Galien and Aristotle, doctors thought that the birth of a son was proof of a good conception, since the man's seed had overcome the woman's.

The preference for boys is not only explained by scientific reasons, but also by socio-economic considerations, especially among the upper classes. A son was, first and foremost, a successor to his father, a girl was a future wife who had to be provided with a dowry and was going to reduce the family fortune. In royal and princely circles, the birth of a son was obviously awaited with great impatience, and the birth of a daughter could sometimes be received with a good deal of disappointment. This is how Guillaume d'Auvergne, bishop of Paris from 1228 to 1249, consoles Saint Louis at the birth of a daughter:

> The queen of France, Marguerite, the wife of King Saint Louis, was just about to have her first child. An heir to the throne was impatiently awaited: she gave birth to a girl. Now came the matter of bearing the bad news to the father. It was a delicate mission: no one in the court wanted to do it. Finally, the good bishop of Paris, Guillaume d'Auvergne was called and begged to carry it out himself, using great care. "I make it my business," he replied. And immediately entering the prince's chamber, he offered him this little discourse:

"Sire, rejoice. I announce to you a very happy event: France has just been enriched with a king. And here is how: if the heavens had given you a son, it would have been necessary for you to cede to him a vast earldom; but you have a daughter: by her marriage, on the contrary, you will win another realm."

The king smiled: he was consoled.[34]

Guillaume d'Auvergne's argument carries weight in the period when the kings of France (in particular, the father of Louis IX) had a tendency to reserve certain rights to the royal domain for younger brothers and to cleverly arrange politically advantageous marriages for their daughters in order to increase their realms.

But all this does not mean that, once she was born, a daughter was less loved than a son. In the accounts of miracles from the twelfth and thirteenth centuries, it is clear that when an accident or illness befalls her, as much care is given to a daughter as would be to a son, and the parents are just as present, active, and efficient when it comes to obtaining miracles for one or the other.[35]

Brothers and Sisters

Because of the limited life expectancy in medieval society, brothers and sisters had a much better chance of living together than children and parents. With parents gone early, sibling bonds were, along with marriage bonds, the strongest ties uniting individuals in the Middle Ages. As age differences were generally slight, brothers often teamed up together in games. In the twelfth- and thirteenth-century miracle accounts, we can find brothers and sisters engaged in games in the courtyard of the house. When the mother leaves the house to go to church or to work, she often leaves the youngest children in the care of the oldest ones, still very young themselves, like the English mother from the end of the twelfth century who goes out to winnow in the courtyard, leaving her two children of a year and a half and three in the bath. She leaves the house with complete confidence, the hagiographer explains, "because the oldest was used to watching over the youngest."[36] At the beginning of the thirteenth century, we find a child of nine years, whose parents are dead, taking care of his brother, his elder by three years, deaf and mute since birth, serving as his guide and interpreter during his pilgrimage and prayers at the tomb of Saint Wulfstan.[37]

But it is much more often the oldest daughter who takes care of her brothers and sisters. We find her tending the youngest one still in the cradle or sewing the clasp back on her little sister's coat. When she belongs to a large working-class family, especially if the mother or father are handicapped, the oldest sister must take charge of the other siblings when she is sometimes still very young. At the end of the thirteenth century, in Saint-Denis, because of her mother's blindness, Emmeline (who is between nine and twelve years old) must take care of her five brothers and sisters. She feeds them and gives them their baths.[38] Some older sisters also play very active roles in the miracles which heal their little brothers and sisters, in certain cases, standing in for the mother.[39]

The affection which links brothers and sisters is always very strong. A hagiographer of Thomas Becket, Benedict of Peterborough, tells us this amusing story from about 1175 of a certain little Beatrice who, "abandoning herself to her amusements and games, as is customary at this age," loses the cheese which has been entrusted to her. Fearing her parents' condemnation, she confesses her secret to one of her brothers who is almost as young as she is, whom she prefers to the others and who is particularly fond of her, hoping to find out if he remembers this event or where the cheese was put down." As her brother, Hugues, cannot remember anything either, they search the house from top to bottom, without success. In fact, Saint Thomas appears to first one and then the other of them in dreams to show them where to find the lost cheese and thus avoid punishment.[40] The double appearance of a saint or the Virgin is always a clear sign of great affection between those who receive the vision.

Sometimes it also happens that the saint appears to the little brother of someone who is ill to tell him to warn his sibling that he must not wait any longer to go to the sanctuary to pray in order to recover his health. Or, again, a very young dead child appears in the dreams of his brother or sister to call him to order: a few days after his revival, Hervé, twelve years old, receives two similar nocturnal visions in which "his little sister who had died immediately after seeing the light of day and who had been baptized" appears to him to remind him that he must honor his vow and go to thank the saint who saved him.[41] To show that this is a case of a favorable apparition, the hagiographer specifies that the little girl had been cleansed of original sin. The baptism of a child is, for the Church, a way of drawing a clear line between good child-ghosts and bad child-ghosts. "In saying this [the little sister] gave her brother a kiss, and from her nostrils came a very sweet scent."

When children grow up, brothers and sisters maintain close relationships. When there is a physical or mental handicap, we often see parents appearing at their "child's" side, even into adulthood. But when the parents are dead or absent from the account, it is the brothers or sisters who play the primary role. There are numerous examples of brothers and sisters who go together to beg for a miracle and who help one another in times of trouble. Amile, a Parisian from the end of the thirteenth century, is paralyzed on the entire right side of her body. Tired of living with an invalid, her husband abandons her. Because she has no resources, she must then beg for a living. Deserted by all, the only person who remains close to her is one of her brothers who takes her to the sanctuary of Saint-Denis.[42] When an adult falls sick or suffers from an accident, in the absence of parents or spouse, it is nearly always brothers and sisters who provide the necessary care. It is also because of these very strong ties that uncles and aunts are such important figures for children.

We must, no doubt, qualify this portrait which can seem a bit idyllic. Sometimes brothers and sisters may quarrel among themselves, refuse to help each other, or even come into real conflict. However, this type of confrontational relationship is the exception in narrative texts. Conflict breaks out primarily when parents die, leading to quarrels over the inheritance among wealthy siblings.

Grandparents

We encounter few grandparents in medieval sources, largely because the life expectancy for adults is low. As men married much later than women (sometimes by as much as ten or fifteen years), they had even less chance than their wives of experiencing the joys of the grandparent. Born in 1214, Saint Louis was the first king of France to know his grandfather, Philippe Auguste, who died of malaria at the age of fifty-seven on July 14, 1223. According to his biographers, Jean de Joinville and Guillaume de Saint-Pathus, during his life, Saint Louis liked to recall his memories of his grandfather introducing him to the government of the realm. To a greater extent than his father, his grandfather no doubt represented to him the ideal model of a French king and the fact of his presence since infancy could have only reinforced his awareness of the continuity of the Capetian dynasty.[43]

Though rare, the testimonies of relationships between grandparents and grandchildren nevertheless demonstrate strong mutual feelings and camaraderie. At the beginning of the fourteenth century, in Montaillou, we find a dead grandmother returning to embrace her grandchildren in their bed. When certain authors recount their childhood memories, they sometimes retain moving remembrances of their grandparents. Thus, in the thirteenth century, Salimbene de Adam writes:

> My father's mother, my grandmother, had for her given name Ermengarda. She was a wise woman, a hundred years old when she died. For fifteen years, I lived with her in my father's house. How many times did she teach me to avoid bad company and choose good company, to be wise, repentant, and good: may God bless her just as many times; because she did so frequently.[44]

Benvenuto Cellini remembers his grandfather like this:

> I was already about three years old; my grandfather Andrea was still alive and was more than a hundred years old. One day when a water pipe was being changed, a very large scorpion came out of it, which no one saw, and which went down another pipe to the ground, where it hid under a bench. I noticed it and ran to pick it up. It was so big that its tail stuck out of one side of my hand, and its pincers out of the other. I ran, I was told, to my grandfather with cries of joy, and I said to him, "Look, Grandfather, see my beautiful crayfish!" Recognizing it to be a scorpion, he almost fell over dead, he loved me so much and was so afraid for me. Cajoling and coaxing me over and over, he asked me to give it to him, but I grasped it all the more tightly and I cried, because I didn't want to give it to anyone.

Finally, it is Cellini's father who, alerted by their cries, arrives to cut the pincers and the tail from the animal with a pair of scissors.[45]

These few accounts are good evidence that when children know their grandfathers or grandmothers, the latter are often very old. They also demonstrate how the grandparent's memory remains alive in the mind of the medieval child, and plays a part in the development of a familial memory.

The Nurse

The figure of the nurse is very present in novelistic accounts, which, for the most part, involve aristocratic circles in which the practice of hiring wet nurses was common, as it also undoubtedly was among the nobility and urban bourgeois at the end of the Middle Ages. But it would be unwise to draw any conclusions from this about their actual importance. In fact, in the great majority of medieval families (the peasantry), nursing was primarily maternal. Already in the Middle Ages, all the great thinkers advocated it.[46] Aldebrandin of Sienna writes, for example, "Know that the milk which must be given to him, and which is worth the most, is that of his mother."[47] And Giles of Rome goes further: "The milk of the mother is the more suited to her child's nature than the milk of another woman."[48] For another doctor of the same period, if the maternal breast is preferable, it was not only because the mother's milk was the best possible nourishment for the child, but also because nursing created a special relationship between the baby and the one who nursed it.

In the Middle Ages, men and women were convinced that, in some hereditary manner, milk transmitted the virtues of the mother and the maternal line. They thought that at the time of birth, blood turned white and became milk (by the process of *dealbation*). Thus, according to medieval beliefs, milk was of the same nature as the blood which nourished the infant in the uterus. Aaleth, the mother of Saint Bernard, "always refused to let her children (six boys and one girl) be fed the milk of a stranger, as if, with her maternal milk, she had to provide them with all the good that could be found in her."[49]

Being obliged, however, to take into account the customs of the bourgeoisie and aristocracy at the end of the Middle Ages, or the inability of certain mothers to nurse, doctors gave much advice regarding the choice of the nurse, so that the values she transmitted to the child would be good ones. According to Aldebrandin of Sienna, it was necessary that she be in the very prime of life, that she resemble the mother, be in good health, and have big and hard breasts so that the milk would be abundant. She must be neither quick-tempered, nor sad, nor fearful, nor stupid. She must also pay careful attention to her diet and abstain from sexual relations during nursing because the danger of becoming pregnant would be too great. In which case, the good blood would go to nourish the fetus, while the bad blood would be transformed into milk. Nursing, either hired or maternal, lasted about two years.

As with all the other ways children were "circulated" in the Middle Ages, putting a child out to nurse must not be interpreted according to our own standards, as a sign of lack of interest in the child. This is true for at least three reasons: it was, first of all, the result of parental concern for the child's well-being;

the parents continued to have, or quickly resumed, a close relationship with their child; and finally, the child in a nurse's care knew no lack of affection, as becomes clear, for example, in the Provençal chanson de geste, *Daurel et Beton*, for the end of the twelfth century:

> Madame Aisileneta [the nurse], whom Jesus blesses, embraces him very gently, as is fitting, then wraps him in a beautiful silk cloth and dresses him in a little ermine skin and then sings him a beautiful song, gazing down on him, her face lowered, and prays to God to give him a long life.[50]

Thus, within the family structure, there is a place for strong emotions. It is not by chance that expressions like "to love as a mother" or "to hold dear as one's son," etc., abound throughout medieval literature. When an author wants to show very great tenderness between two beings, he often evokes the feelings of parent and child by way of comparison.

Bagpipes; two boys with shields, riding a donkey and a dog, tilt at each other. Ms. Bodl. 264, fol. 50.

A game of bowls. Boy on right bowls towards left, where there are two balls and a boy stooping over them. In center, another ball, with boy moving away. We are told that this game is played in Australia and is called 'Duck shooting or poison ball; the aim being to hit opponents below the knee. Ms. Bodl. 264, fol. 63.

Two boys on stilts. The stilts are lop-sided and about a foot high. Ms. Bodl. 264, fol. 65.

Three boys playing with swing, which hangs from a pulley. Ms. Bodl. 264, fol. 78v.

Hunting the hunter. A human-sized hare carries off a boy, who is trussed up and tied to a stick; another hare stretches his bow. A seated hare looks at a boy who has taken refuge in a tree. Ms. Bodl. 264, fol. 81v.

Boy and girl play a board game called 'merelles' or nine men's morris. Ms.Bodl.264, fol.112.

Four girls play blind man's buff. Three of them tease the 'blind man' by hitting her with knotted hoods. Ms .Bodl. 264, fol. 130v.

A horse standing on his hindlegs, and playing a drum with his forelegs. A boy holds the drum. Ms. Bodl. 264, fol. 96v.

THE CHILD
in
SOCIETY

Twelfth–Early Sixteenth Centuries

Danièle Alexandre-Bidon

After a good thirteenth century, the two hundred years which followed were marked by upheavals which the family structure could not escape. We see the family torn to shreds by the great plagues, the support system disrupted for the time by the horrible fear of contagion. Contemporaries testify to this, like Boccaccio in the introduction to his *Decameron:*

> Brother abandoned brother, uncle nephew, sister brother, often even the wife her husband. And here is something even worse and scarcely believable. Fathers and mothers avoided going to see and to help their children, as if their children were no longer their own.

And nevertheless, at the close of this demographic disaster, nothing had fundamentally changed. If we are to believe the images which multiplied exponentially in the fifteenth century, children were just as loved and protected as before. The texts, no matter what they are, do not contradict this. Pedagogical literature, which experienced an unprecedented revival in the thirteenth century,[1] was enriched once more in the fourteenth century with Italian humanism. The nursery, already earlier established in the thirteenth century, was perfected. Cradles were made more comfortable—the rocking cradle and hood were invented—and came into wide use among the populace. All that is now common knowledge.[2]

With the crises of the late Middle Ages, a part of the ancient family regained an important role: uncles or grandparents replaced lost parents; adult brothers often became responsible for their unmarried sisters, and it fell to the son to take in his mother, if she so desired, or to otherwise provide for her. The same was true for children who, it was believed, ought to benefit from the protective presence of grandmothers. Finally, family life lasted longer than ever, at least for male children who often remained at home until they were almost thirty years old. The model of the marital family must be understood in its larger sense: it included children, all children, whoever they were, not only brothers and sisters, who already made the family large, but children from the outside. In Italy, when adolescents, indeed even children, were married, the young couple took up residence in the parents' home. Throughout, wives were advised to accept husbands' bastard children into the bosom of the family—the opposite was not true. In the Mediterranean, young slaves, bought on the eastern borders of Europe or even Africa, were added to the children and bastards. The desire for children no doubt grew out of marrying so late, especially for men, and the great demographic difficulties of the fourteenth century. The number of children increased again. An average of five children could be found living in each home. In the French realm, which no doubt counted sixteen million inhabitants before the great plague—and some historians even place the figure at twenty—of which nearly 90 percent were peasants, there were, as a consequence, millions of children.[3]

Within this marital, but ample, family unit at the end of the Middle Ages, the child grew up. While no doubt spending all his early years relatively overprotected, he was also expected to pitch in, sometimes *stricto sensu*. Like every member of the family, he had a role to play, a role much better known than in the preceding period. The sources which tell us about children are clearly more abundant for last three centuries of the Middle Ages than for any that came before. The images of and remarks on early life become too numerous to count. This concrete information, more precise than ever before, prompts historians to enlarge upon all aspects of the child's daily life. First of all, it allows us to unveil the life of the very young and of the nursery,[4] then, to examine the child's place and mode of existence in medieval society.[5] Finally, sources from the late Middle Ages allow us to enter new domains, two of which are of primary importance for the history of the child: schooling, which increased dramatically in the thirteenth century, and putting children to work, be it at home or in the family enterprise or with other families, as apprentices, for instance, among the commoners, or as pages among the nobility.

SIX

Working within
the Family

We will never know at exactly what age children were actually put to work, especially in rural areas. No doubt they helped their parents with farm tasks from the time that they were very young. That is certainly what we would guess from legal sources. To begin to examine the work of children, we need not distinguish between those living in town and those living in the country. In the Middle Ages, there was no separation of this kind. Peasants lived in the town, which they left each morning to go to work in the "outskirts," and many trades were practiced in the country as well as in the towns.

An Early and Gradual Introduction

In the eyes of medieval educators, entering the world of work at a young age represented, in some way, security for life. As the thirteenth-century Catalan, Raymond Lulle, says, "rather than leaving him an inheritance of money or possessions, there is no better way to ensure a son wealth than by enriching him through an apprenticeship in a trade," and, according to Philippe de Novare, "one must teach children whatever trade suits them best; and one must begin as early as possible."[1] Beginning young was a guarantee of success. However, it was only gradually that children, destined to succeed their parents, were introduced into the economic activities of the latter, whether they were peasants or artisans of the towns. Professional initiation began, first of all, with toys designed for children, such as the tea sets made by potters which have been found in great number in excavations of large cities. Some bear traces of burning, which allow us to imagine that little girls and boys—cooking was a masculine occupation—practiced their mother's recipes over the fire. Autobiographical accounts confirm this. The fourteenth-century chronicler and poet, Froissart[2] recalls that he amused himself by playing baker and preparing small tarts, flans, and little rolls to bake in an oven built out of four tiles. He also constructed miniature mills and waterworks for fun. Other children built sand castles or abbeys, or learned to perform the mass with the help of a small altar and miniature accessories, according to the future in store for them. In the twelfth century, little Guibert de Nogent, committed to the religious life, was dressed as a cleric by his tutor; even costumes were considered instructive. The life of the child consisted partly of preparation for adulthood, through play, and especially through playful imitation.

But, as images reveal, very young children primarily accompanied their parents to the workplace, where they could be supervised and introduced to the practices of their trade at the same time. Thus we see the butcher's son blowing up the bladder of a pig which his father has given to him, girls and boys watching the butcher setting about to burn the beast's bristles, or observing by the doorway as animals are slaughtered. Watching parents work is the second stage of apprenticeship into a trade. In the images, we witness small children helping to press wine, playing with the grape clusters, and trying to climb into the vat with their father, or running alongside the plow, in danger of getting crushed, as they watch him work. If we examine the collections of miracle accounts, it seems clear that children very often accompanied adults to work. In rural areas, farm equipment was responsible for many accidents in the first years of life: children falling into brewery vats, under the wheels of flour or water mills, under the hoofs of pack animals or the donkey turning the millstone.[3] Children also watched their mothers feeding the chickens, collecting eggs, preparing cheese, and picking vegetables. No doubt they learned very early to recognize garden and medicinal plants (simples*). This attentive observation of parental activity was no doubt accompanied by all sorts of advice. The transmission of knowledge among peasant populations culminated when the father took his son to market to be "initiated into market life and customs," as it says in the thirteenth-century fabliau, *Vilain de Farbus*.[4]

Many examples lead us to believe that this introduction into a profession began as soon as a child acquired a certain mastery in speech, or an initial introduction to schooling, thus quite early. Even before the age of five, a child could be considered old enough not only to learn by observing a parent's actions and techniques, but also to act as a credible witness of commercial transactions. In his essay on the businessman in the Middle Ages, Jean Favier[5] gives the example of a young woman called to testify about the repayment of a debt, an event which took place when she was only four years old:

> Jeanne de Clés said under oath that it was a good twenty-six years ago that the mother, Agnès la Patinière had the woad dyestuff all ready to put in the vat, the aforementioned dyestuff which Sire Jean [Broinbroke, rich cloth merchant of Douai] took in payment for the debt that Marion owed him. She did not know what the debt was, but she saw the woad measured out. She was four years old, and heard her mother ask Sire John for twenty pounds for the rest of the purchase of this dyestuff. And Sire John said, "Old Gossip, I don't know what I owe you, but I will put you in my will. . . ."

The third stage of practical initiation into professional life consisted of helping parents with daily tasks in whatever small ways children could. All the safest activities were assigned to children. Boys and girls participated in the upbringing of the younger children, housework, and baby-sitting. The sons of carpenters collected the wood shavings used to heat the house. Gathering kindling and carrying firewood were two of the boyhood chores most frequently represented by illuminators. Other boys collect chestnuts which an adult roasts, as we see in medicinal plant books, or gather acorns from an oak which has been cut down. Still others go along with their father to cut the grape vines in March, as shown on the sculpted calendar of Mimizan.[6] Little boys climbed trees to pick cherries, almonds, or olives, and helped their mothers in the garden. Gardening, moreover, was a traditional childhood activity, in the country as well as in medieval monasteries where child-monks, sometimes of peasant origin, passed their free time not only playing, but also tending their vegetable patches: that is what the tenth-century English pedagogical text, the *Colloque* of Aelfric Bata, tells us. The young also helped their mothers with fetching water and making cloth. They helped wind the skeins of wool or hemp. They were responsible for serving drinks at the table: they went to get wine from the cellars. Children of both sexes were often charged with bringing a meal to their father, still in the fields during the harvest, or shut up in the leper-house, as in the novel, *Ami et Amile*. In town, an empty shopping bag over his shoulder, the youngest son accompanies the oldest, or his parents, as they do their errands.

Thus, children were put to work very young, but even so, they were not "exploited" according to our modern standards, at least not before adolescence. Indeed, thirteenth-century doctors and educators such as Philippe de Novare propose that "from the ages of seven to twelve, children should not undertake heavy and difficult work, so that their growth should not be hampered." This interval was surely not based on physiological grounds alone. Twelve is a symbolic number which calls up completion: there are twelve apostles, twelve months in a year, twelve *derniers* in a *sou*, and twelve years to complete childhood. We might wonder how widespread such ideas were among the general populace, but in the fifteenth century, in a letter to his wife, dated June 27, 1465, the Englishman John Paston reminds her that "every poor man who has brought up his children until they reached twelve years of age usually finds that, at this age, they can help him and be of some use to him."[7] But to contemporaries, this "usefulness" was sometimes like "servitude."

Servitude?

Indeed, some children did suffer from being forced to work under difficult conditions. In fifteenth-century Auvergne, we see a mother and her ten-year-old son salvaging the broken roofs of abandoned houses and reselling beams and tiles.[8] In Provence, "hired hands, frail women, young girls, and poor children" were hired as "cheap labor" to pull up weeds which invaded the fields of woad.[9] It was especially among these kinds of children, unprotected by work contracts and obliged to slave at their parents' sides to survive, that we surely find traces of miserably spent youths. Even twelve-year-old children could be charged with difficult chores, such as lugging water, which they did routinely with their mothers. In a strange way, a child's small stature was sometimes the unfortunate reason he was assigned certain dangerous tasks: young miners were employed to hollow out narrow clay tunnels, as in the fourteenth century in the Montagne

Noir. Their footprints have been found in the clay of the Caleil cave. Others were engaged to clean out wells, as when the sixteenth-century lord of Gouberville makes a child whom he calls "the little Englishman" descend into the depths of his wells, seated in a bucket.

It is impossible, however, to estimate what proportion of children lived under such duress. Without a doubt, the figure is low. As a general rule, the young were not deprived of their childhood. First of all, children played as they worked. As we know from legal sources, young cowherds chatted and amused themselves with stick games while they watched the cattle. In *Aucassin et Nicolette*, we witness young shepherds buying—with Nicolette's money—"cakes, knives in their sheaths, flutes, cornets, batons, and pipes" to amuse themselves.[10] Moreover, in urban circles, indeed even among rich peasants, not all children were called upon to work. Those belonging to well-to-do rural families or the bourgeoisie might escape work if their parents took in a young valet or a little servant girl. That is exactly the situation we find in a song by Colin Muset, from the middle of the thirteenth century. In this song, the father returns from work, and everyone smothers him with attention:

> My boy [valet] is going to water
> My horse and take care of it
> My maid [young servant girl] is going to kill
> Two capons to serve
> In garlic sauce.
> My daughter brings me a comb
> In her hand out of courtesy:
> Thus am I lord of my mansion
> More than anyone could say![11]

The romance, *Courtois d'Arras*, from the same period, considers the case of a younger brother exempted from working on the farm, at the expense of the elder brother who accuses his father of exploiting him "while my brother gets off easy" and complains throughout the poem, "He's my younger brother, he's smaller than I am . . . you treat me like your slave."[12] After the eldest runs away, it is the youngest son's turn to complain of constantly waiting upon his father, "night and day, like a domestic servant," "a slave" ("*vostre serf*" reads the text), or "domestic" ("*vallet*"), who "*serf*" (serves, as a serf) his father without relief. Such was the experience of young men like these in difficult positions on the farm. Before their marriages, which were often late, and which finally allowed them to establish themselves independently, young men no doubt deeply resented their lack of autonomy. But these latter were no longer children. They belonged to that other age group, young people, about which a new collection of articles has just appeared.[13]

Boys in the Fields

The everyday life of the young peasant was not terribly easy, as we witness in this romance. Early in the morning, the father goes to shake his son Courtois awake:

Up, my son! you've slept a long time:
At this hour, your lambs ought to
Have already grazed in the short grass.
Father, you are going to work me to death:
Late to bed and early to rise,
That is the life I have always led.

The main task of the young boy was to get rid of predators that threatened the crops, to kill toads and large insects in the garden, and to protect the vegetable patch. Thus, according to Pierre de Crescens, a learned Italian agronomist of the thirteenth century, it was the children who hunted maybugs and who, armed with slingshots during the sowing season or posted in vineyards before the grape harvest, hunted birds:

> If there were so many birds attacking the vines that scarecrows were not sufficient, it was necessary to build a little hut on four posts in the middle of the vineyard and put a child in it. He pulled on cords fastened to poles outside and around the vineyard. They were attached to the inside of the hut, and there were bells attached to the poles. He made them ring by pulling the cords and also banged on sticks, gourds, and other noisemakers from there where he could see the birds.[14]

Boys were first put to work with their father, harvesting the rape with him, as in Montaillou.[15] They accompanied him to the fields to do the sowing, to carry sheaves of wheat to the wagon, or to lead the horse harnessed to the harrow. They used all their strength to hold the sheep's back legs during shearing, as we see in a fifteenth-century missal illumination.* Much of their activity involved the livestock, and thus they were often left to themselves during the day. A young shepherd who later became well known, Jean de Brie, wrote a book for King Charles V—later lost and which we only know through an abridged version from the early sixteenth century—entitled *Le Bon berger* [The Good Shepherd].[16] Listed there are childhood tasks, from the most simple to the most difficult, which he himself performed. At eight years old, a boy was "appointed and delegated to watch the geese and the goslings" for six months, then, to watch the pigs, and finally, at about nine or ten years, to lead the horses at the plow. It is at this same age, nine years and four months to be exact, that Matthäus Schwarz, a young urban runaway, earns his livelihood watching a herd of cattle with a young peasant.[17] In general, it was at about this age that the first work accidents took place. Jean de Brie was not an exception to the rule. Leading the plow horses, he suffers from a crushed foot, and then he has another accident when he is watching a herd of ten dairy cows. Next comes the age of responsibilities. At eleven years old, he watches 80 sheep, at fourteen, 200 ewes: thus entire living fortunes were entrusted to pre-adolescents. Young peasants also led the pigs to hunt acorns. These animals were dangerous, and we find, in a book of miracles from Notre-Dame de Soissons, a young "swineherd" of nine years, injured in the leg and supported by his mother, presenting his wound to the Virgin. Legal sources and accounts verify lines to them in her *Book of the Three Virtues*, a treatise on comportment. We can, however, recognize certain kinds of behavior they shared with the nobility and the bourgeoisie. Thus, the "reserve" of Joan of Arc is recommended to girls in all social classes. On the other hand, the more verbose bourgeoisie expressed itself as early as the thirteenth century on the upbringing of urban youth, to whom the Italian, Bonvoisin Da La Riva, even dedicated a book of good manners, the *Fifty Courtesies of the Table*,[26] in which he requests that the young reader not be "boorish" and to restrain from "being naughty." Despite these points in common, the ways of peasants were undoubtedly not those of townspeople.

The Children of Merchants

In town, the children of storekeepers and merchants led a more privileged existence. More comfortable living conditions were indeed available to urban dwellers, as well as services less frequently found in the country. That is the case with school. In town, there were many children. In the thirteenth–fourteenth centuries, there were already some large cities. If Arras, Avignon, Beauvais, Bourges, or Lyon counted only 10,000 to 20,000 inhabitants, Paris might have had 200,000. There were many cities which contained 25,000 to 35,000 residents, such as Strasbourg, Narbonne, Toulouse, Tours, or Orléans, or even more than that, like Rouen or Montpellier.[27] In the fourteenth and fifteenth centuries, the inhabitants of towns represented 10 to 15 percent of the population. Under these flourishing urban conditions, in large enterprises and small family businesses alike, a place was soon found for children. Beginning from the time they reached the age of reason, boys were willingly given responsibilities. In Auvergne in the fifteenth century, a child "of eight to ten years" sold candles all by himself, and the children of a cloth shearer watched the store in their father's absence: they must have already known how to count.[28] Indeed, city children, and especially those of merchants, attended the little schools which opened in every neighborhood. No doubt it was their relatively protected way of life that led some clerics and strict educators to urge their parents to give them a more austere upbringing. At the end of the fourteenth century, Dominici, a Florentine, suggests providing boys with only "a coarse diet":

> Let them walk barefoot; accustom them to hard work and strengthen their bodies so that, if the necessity arises, they can be content with little. . . . Let them sleep, at least once a week, seated, completely dressed, and with the window opened, and get them used to fasting. In short, treat them like the children of a peasant.

As for their sisters, he says, "it doesn't matter how you feed a girl, as long as she stays alive. She doesn't need to be fat." It is doubtful that parents obeyed his injunctions, which do, however, give a good idea of childhood duties:

> Teach her all the household chores: to bake bread, roast capon, sift flour, do the cooking, the washing, make the beds; to spin and to weave French purses; to embroider on silk, to make clothes out of cloth and wool; to fit

soles to shoes and to do all similar things so that, when you give her away in marriage, men do not say, "she's from a land of savages!"[29]

In reality, girls and boys were not maltreated. This discrepancy between the vituperations of clerics and the actual situation no doubt resulted from an innate mistrust on the part of the Church toward those who earned money. Doubtlessly, they deemed it necessary to keep a closer eye on their off-spring, too protected and, according to them, constantly tempted by a life of indolence. They did not hesitate to give parents strong words of advice—but, for the most part, after the fact—on their intellectual training. Clerics and scholars were offended by the idea of opening learning to men of commerce. Gilles Le Muisit, a Parisian author from the beginning of the fourteenth century, thought that the laity should not be educated, and that it would be better for them to learn "*marcheandise*," or commerce. That did not stop certain rich merchants from being "literate," that is, from knowing Latin, and even Greek, which they learned as children. Thus, in Aix, at the beginning of the fourteenth century, a Jewish grandmother, a well-to-do merchant, decides to bequeath her books to her grandson—on the condition that he learn Latin. If, in the fifteenth century, a bankrupt merchant from Lyon, François Garin, decides that his adolescent son must, above all, learn "to count well," he also proposes that he learn Latin grammar and that he read an ancient moral treatise, Boethius' *Consolation*.

Sent to school early, as in Venice, "according to the custom of the city," children learned to read and write quickly, and then spent a few months on arithmetic or the study of specialized manuals, such as the *Cri des monnoyes*, a text printed in Paris about 1506, before being put to work at the bank, if they were gifted. Thus, children were engaged in the Strozzi-Guineldi clothing business in Florence in 1464, as retail sellers or cashiers.[30] Merchants appreciated precocious children. It was at the age of ten that Messer Giannozzo Manetti, who would become a powerful merchant and political figure in Florence, found himself in charge of the cash accounts. At fourteen, when they came of age, merchants' sons aspired to confronting the realities of business life. At this age, the young Schwarz became his father's representative in the buying and selling of wine, which he tasted with professional skill before announcing his intention to purchase it. Imagine what confidence fathers had to have in their sons to allow them to assume such important tasks so young. Business sense also led merchants of different countries to send their sons on travel exchanges, so that they could increase their knowledge and learn foreign languages. Adolescents were no more hesitant than they are today to cross Europe or the seas, like Hans Wessel, the young Hanseatic boy, who, from the ages of twelve to twenty, made seven long sea journeys, one each year.[31] At the end of the fifteenth century, they were not even afraid to cross the Atlantic, like the son of Christopher Columbus who "at the very young age of thirteen years," accompanied his father on his last voyage. All these young boys ran the risk of being shipwrecked or even of being taken hostage: merchants were sometimes obliged to entrust their sons to the Moors as a guarantee in order to be able to follow their routes.[32] And such formative journeys sometimes lasted many years.

room and bed, and footwear."[5] If they sometimes promised to send the apprentice to school, this type of clause seems to have applied more often to boys than to girls. In Montpellier, one contract out of three provides for the instruction of boys, as opposed to only one out of five for girls.[6] Moreover, this instruction was limited: "until he has learned his ABC's and seven psalms (of penitence), and he has been tonsured, and sent to learn to write for the period of two months." The young Guillaume Rouleau, eight years old, who is the object of so much concern here, is a cooper's apprentice.[7] With a clear sense of symmetry, his master promises him a builder's tool and a compass at the end of his eleven years of training, which, we can clearly see, were not devoted entirely to cooperage. At the end of the Middle Ages, the merchant also had to know how to read and write. These relatively privileged conditions must not allow us to forget that the young apprentice had as many duties as rights. Among the Aix potters, in 1517, if an apprentice fell ill, he had to reimburse his master for his food, medicine, and the doctor's fees, and guarantee that he would make up double the work time lost. We tremble at the sense of these children's schedules we get from reading, in all the contracts, the master's obligation to allow them enough sleep. In Florence, it was forbidden to make apprentices employed in the wool industry work before daybreak—which surely indicates that the practice was very widespread. The young, for that matter, were subjected to the same schedule as adults, and, like everyone else in the medieval world, rose at daybreak. For example, about 1250, weavers began work when the first mass was sung.

Less often, and this is just as disturbing, the master is obligated to treat the child "gently," or even to not hit him on the head—which surely implies that he is allowed to hit other parts of the body. We begin to hope that the guilds' supervision was effective enough to prevent overexploitation and maltreatment. In any case, masters promised not to be abusive, "not to have him do what is beyond his strength," as we can read in a weaver's hand in one Genoese contract. Excesses took place, however. But the young had legal recourse, and apprentices who were beaten could denounce their masters and win their court cases. Thus, in England in 1371, two brothers appear before the court to request that their apprenticeship contract be broken. They accuse their master of being absent for a long time without providing for their training, which is serious, and they accuse his wife of not giving them enough food and beating them "so wickedly" that one of them has lost his left eye from it. A medical examination follows, provides evidence of the maltreatment, and the investigation reveals that the master, in fact, was in jail "and that neither he nor his wife could stand the boys."[8] But no honest master wished to find himself in such an embarrassing situation with regard to his colleagues. It was in no one's interest to mistreat apprentices, who constituted a cheap labor force. Undoubtedly, most apprenticeships worked out to the satisfaction of both parties.

Finally, no matter what the type of activity, it seems as though masters universally applied the same method: children were put to work gradually. As with work at home, training began with the young watching adults work, in order that they could learn their manual techniques. Tools were put in their hands. As shown in a sixteenth-century engraving, a very small, barefooted boy plays in an ore extractor's workshop with a miniature hammer, imitating the adults. Similarly, the young helped with "small jobs," otherwise known as thankless labor, cleaning the workshop, collecting wood shavings for the carpenter, for example, or carrying in fuel and tending the fire for trades that required it. For making mortar, the young swept up the dust, cleaned the canvases after they were used, and set them out to dry. In 1464, we find children assigned to the post of "supervising the workers" for an Italian weaver.[9] They no doubt profited by observing the weavers' movements. When apprentices began to apply their knowledge, they practiced on easy projects. Thus, the little potters of Burgundy are only allowed to throw lids on the potter's wheel, and not pots. For apprentice painters, in the twelfth century, the monk Théophile explains that "it is gradually, bit by bit, that the arts are taught. The painter must first learn to make the colors," then "to apply his mind to mixing them." Boccaccio makes gentle fun of his first lessons in the sixth story of the sixth day of his *Decameron*: the children begin to make pictures in which "the right eye is bigger than the left; elsewhere, it is lower. This is the way children first draw faces when they receive their first lessons." Later, they apply themselves seriously to copying the models found in artist notebooks. In an ink drawing done in about 1140–1150,[10] a very young apprentice, whose name is Everwin and who looks to be about eight or ten years old, works at the feet of his master painting arabesques and acanthus leaves. Learning to reproduce ornamental motifs no doubt constituted the first stage of drawing lessons. This gradual introduction was even more necessary for apprenticeships in the medical professions, in which some techniques could be life threatening to the client. Doctors' apprentices carried the precious glass urinal, carefully packed in a willow container. Barbers' apprentices were content to hold the bowl of blood during an operation; in this way, they got used to the sight of blood. In the same way, the young assistants of surgeons were responsible for the ewer and towel used for washing hands after the operation.

Women's Occupations

What did girls do? Primarily, they worked in the textile trades, as dressmakers, linen maids, or embroiderers. Like Marion, eleven years old, they worked making linen cloth.[11] But sometimes, parents tried to have their daughters acquire very specialized training: weaving wide ribbon or silk, embroidering the edges of caps, or, in Italy, French purses, and in Spain, even the art of "Portuguese folds." Girls also worked in the food trades. Thus, in Montpellier, we find that most bakery or pastry shop apprentices are girls rather than boys.[12] Some of them went to work for doctors, artists, and scribes.[13] But all young girls did not have access to such professions. A number of them, orphans without mothers, were simply placed by their fathers as young servants with clergymen of good reputation or with members of the bourgeoisie who undertook, by "agreement," to care for and to marry the child "at the suitable age," that is, about fifteen or sixteen years old. That was the case, in 1425, with a "poor farmer" from Toulouse, artist of northern France, belonged to a family full of artists; his father, son, and nephew were painters, his daughter, an "illuminatress."[26]

However, in the second stage, young artists often left their apprenticeships at home for more specialized training. Daughters were not content to learn the craft with their fathers and brothers. They were placed with artists, like that young painter apprenticed to a widow in Montpellier in 1387.[27] Some of them became well known, like the daughter of the illuminator, Jean le Noir, Bourgot, who worked for the king of France. Some medieval manuscripts done by children still exist, and they are sometimes signed or include some colophon revealing the child's age. And when, to our attentive but untrained eye, an illumination seems crude, it is sometimes the case that an eleven-year-old child produced it. Indeed, many illuminators began work at a young age. Children worked with scribes as well, and in manuscript illustrations, portraits of the author show both the principal scribe and his apprentice, seated at his feet, holding out his ink and trimming his quill pens for him. And we have even more direct evidence of these young ones at work: they expressed themselves on the parchment of the books that they copied. Indeed, beginning from the twelfth century, manuscript colophons attest to the existence of apprentices. The spirit of youth did not submit happily to sitting still for long hours copying, and the apprentice did not hesitate to leave signs of his displeasure. Thus, in Italy, in about 1473–1474, a young Jewish apprentice from the province of Ancone, copying a *Book of Instruction*, draws some pictures of women in red ink, and, pleased with himself, inscribes under them, "I am a good painter-apprentice." Moreover, he amuses himself by scribbling jokes and *"vers de mirliton"* in the margins of this book, which is no doubt too serious in his eyes, making reference to his apprenticeship:

> Blessed is the one who gives strength to the one who is worn out
> My eyes had gone dark and my brain was exhausted
> To the point that I had become motionless and overwhelmed!
> But I found vigor and sure agility,
> Laboring at my task, attentive to my work,
> Me, the fool, bursting with stupidity.[28]

This example, which is autobiographical and captures something of real life, demonstrates how apprenticeships were not necessarily experienced as a burdensome duty, but rather, as self-discovery, and that, when they entered the world of work, young people did not lose their youthful spirit.

Exploited Children or Youth in Training?

What did all these children earn by working this way? Not much. The oldest apprentices sometimes received a salary. But most of them were only considered unskilled wage-earners. As a general rule, the young were underpaid, as were women. "For equal work, unequal wages," says Alessandro Stella with regard to Italian "store children."[29] Very unequal wages, indeed: two to sixteen florins per year, while an adult received eighteen to thirty-three. An adolescent of fourteen could make a third of the salary an adult made. However this salary, so inadequate at first glance, seems to have been attractive enough to draw young people from long distances to seek positions with masters offering it. This lower remuneration for young workers was an old custom. A little riddle taken from an arithmetic book attributed to Alcuin and composed for the edification—and amusement—of his royal pupil, Pepin, *Figures and Mathematical Subtleties*, already demonstrates this discrepancy:

> Six workers are engaged in building a house. Among them, there is one apprentice. The five men divide the salary of 25 deniers per day, less the salary of the apprentice, *which represents half the salary of each worker.* How much will each of them receive?[30]

Thus, the late Middle Ages retained this ancient practice which devalued the work of the beginner and of the young in general. But is this salary really as unfair as it seems to be? As an apprentice, one was also fed and housed, which is not generally taken into account, and one certainly considered oneself a "student" more than a worker. Furthermore, we can observe among the weavers of Florence in the fifteenth century that children's pay varied according to their experience. The beginner, between nine and thirteen years old, earned less than the confirmed apprentice, between fourteen and sixteen years old.[31] Given these circumstances, to be less well paid than others might not have been cause for bitter feelings. Moreover, remuneration was often forthcoming at the end of training, more in kind than in money, however: gifts of clothes or shoes, indeed even tools of the trade, as in Spain in the thirteenth century. Thus, we know of the case of a little girl from Seville, ten years old, placed in an apprenticeship with a family on the condition that, at the end of the contract, she should be provided with a weaving loom, so that she, in turn, could set herself up to work.[32] It seems difficult to estimate the value of such gifts. Shoes in the Middle Ages were not worth a great deal. Clothes, on the other hand, were more costly. As to tools of the trade, which were worth the weight of their metal, they often held more symbolic than real value. Supplied with these tools, apprentices could offer proof of the quality and nature of their training to potential employers. Couldn't this have been the equivalent of a diploma at the end of studies? In the cases of trades with complex equipment, such as weaving, a gift of the principal tool, the weaving loom, at the end of the contract, was certainly not an insignificant asset which the child then added to her dowry.

Finally, if children were underpaid, indeed even unpaid, we must understand that this was sometimes what their parents wanted. That was exactly the case with the young Benvenuto Cellini, who entered an apprenticeship in a silversmith's workshop at fifteen. In his autobiography, he recalls the circumstances and the reasons for this choice: "My father did not want me to be paid a salary, like the other apprentices. The reason he gave was that I was doing this out of my own desire to learn the trade; actually, he wanted me to pursue the possibility of drawing." In this specific case, the unpaid apprentice retained a certain amount of freedom. Benvenuto had the right to take time from his workday to devote himself to other activities, drawing, in this case, and to return to his father's house "to play the flute or the cornet."[33] This type of apprenticeship could thus correspond, in this particular instance at least, to an education "à la carte." Alternatively, even though he had at his disposal cheap, not to say, free labor, by not paying them, the master no doubt figured he was reimbursing himself for the work spoiled by novice apprentices. In Italy, artisans complain in the *Florentine Treatise on the Art of Silk*[34] about the imperfections in fabrics worked on by children. Furthermore, to have an apprentice to train always constituted additional work.

A Stolen Childhood?

However, in the Middle Ages, child labor was not considered a burden children had to bear, but training meant to secure them work, a family, and a house as adults, "a bonus given to the young . . . which required certain sacrifices on the part of parents."[35] But it is true that we only hear from the employers. And at the age when, today, one is free from all material constraints, one was, at that time, subjected to the rhythms of adult work. Showing through the written records, however, is the degree of freedom and play which remained to the very young. Before adolescence, little apprentices seem to have had exactly the same childhood freedoms as today. Some of them went to school. They played; if they were not entertaining themselves, they were entertained. They joked—we find proof of this in the manuscripts they copied, in the farces which the writers of those days relate: the little bank employees abandon their posts to release a mouse into the market place.[36] They have scuffles in the workshops. King René had gift boxes given out at Christmas, so that his young kitchen servants could go play dice. The young had some freedom, for example, the freedom to play the flute on holidays to earn money—which was then shared, it is true, with one's master, as in Arles at the end of the Middle Ages.[37] If the apprentice's workday was long, we do not know if he was given breaks and if, as at school or in the monastery, he was not allowed time for "recreation." Furthermore, the fate of the apprentice depended upon many factors. Thus, little female orphans, who were placed very young as servants or chambermaids and who no longer had fathers to protect them, were the easy targets of rapists, sometimes their employers. Beginning from ten or eleven years old, no doubt as soon as they reached puberty (and even though the violation of young girls was relatively rare,[38] because childhood was sacred), this was occasionally the fate of this or that young dressmaker or embroidery apprentice,[39] or farm girl. Marie Ribon, a young orphan of thirteen years, found herself pregnant by her master, and Marion Lévesque, employed to wash dishes, was violated regularly in the barn by her employer, a fifty-year-old laborer.[40] Thus, placing a young girl as a priest's servant,[41] like that "poor little girl," twelve years old, in Montaillou, was no doubt the best way to protect them against the potential cruelty and harassment of a patron.

The fate of the apprentice also depended upon the nature of the activity. The textile trades had a long-standing reputation for demanding hard work. On the other hand, as Franco Franceschi very judiciously remarked,[42] a "shop child," employed to keep accounts, who went home to his family every night, was not subjected to very difficult living conditions. At the end of the Middle Ages, merchants did not want their young brought up too harshly. In the fifteenth century, the Italian, Giovanni Rucellai, advocates simply "letting (the young) run and jump, play tennis and ball."[43] Benvenuto Cellini, who entered an apprenticeship in a silversmith's workshop in 1505 at the age of fifteen, remembers his first work not as a trial but as a pleasure, feeling welcome in a studio where, moreover, the master silversmith "had one son, his only child, whom he ordered many times to help me." Benvenuto, who remembers being "so goodwilled " about his service, speaks of this silversmith as an "excellent man and master."[44]

Little Slaves

There exists one final category of children put to work far away from their families: slaves. From distant countries, sometimes African, more often Turkish or Slavic—hence the etymology of "slave"—the medieval merchant willingly brought back children in his cargo, bought for a small fortune and much in demand in Italy, Sicily, and even in southern France.[45] In the fourteenth and fifteenth centuries, white slaves were the clear majority. The Church authorized their acquisition provided they were infidels—a guideline far from being systematically observed, since we also know of cases of slaves whose mothers were good Christians. These, at least, benefited from a special statute, as did those born north of Corfu.[46] In addition to the Moors and Turks, bought rather as luxury objects and curiosities, there were Tartar children, Turkistans, Russians, and children from the Caucasus, sometimes sold by their own parents, who were transported to Italy in the lower decks of Genoese ships. In the fifteenth century, the Turks sold Serbian, Bulgarian, Hungarian, and Bosnian slaves to Italian bourgeoisie. To procure very young women and little girls, who were a particularly sought-after commodity—up to 90 percent of slave sales in Italy—merchants did not hesitate to obtain them from still other places: little Albanians or Greeks, twelve years old, were sold at Chios; at the end of the fifteenth century, slaves were acquired from the Canaries.[47] Each year, in Genoa, many thousands of eastern or Slavic girls and young women debarked to be sold by the bourgeois Italian merchants; this was not an insignificant population.

Young children were bought willingly, no doubt because they got used to living with their new families and were not tempted to run away or rebel, while at the same time being big enough to help the mistress of the house with domestic work. They were sometimes less than twelve or thirteen years old. We know their ages from sales or health care agreements, because they sometimes arrived in poor health, and the buyer then engaged a doctor to care for them. In Palermo, in 1323, Nicolaus, a twelve-year-old Greek child from Romania, suffered from an infected wound on the arch of his foot, a little boy named Silvester, nine years old, was incontinent. Such care was not given only out of kindness: incontinence constituted a classic case of a broken contract.[48] Magherita Datini, the wife of a great merchant and banker, spoke in her letters of her "herd of juveniles," free and enslaved, who made up her household staff, and her husband regularly ordered new ones to add to their company:

> I pray you, buy me a little slave girl, young and rustic, from eight to ten years old, who is of good stock and robust enough to bear hard work, in good health and of good character so that I can train her as I please. I will only employ her to wash the dishes and carry the wood and the bread to the communal oven and other jobs of this sort.[49]

How did these deported children live? Even if cases of maltreatment were inevitable, the little slaves seem to have become part of the family. They were well taken care of in order to protect the labor force—and the investment—which they represented. A slave child was not a cheap acquisition; in the first third of the fourteenth century, in Italy, a young Tartar was bought from Catalan merchants for the price of a mule, a little girl of ten or twelve years old, acquired at the Venice market, was worth fifty ducats.[50] But their market value does not explain everything. Their buyers paid attention to their clothes and to their games and a "very great indulgence" seems to have been accorded them.[51] That did not keep their families from working them hard. Most often they served as domestics, and did not receive a salary in exchange for their good and loyal services, anymore than young free servants did, for that matter, who were only lodged, clothed, and fed. In reality, if their legal status put them on the margins of society, their living conditions were scarcely different from those of young employees who were legally free. Some young slaves were even particularly well treated, notably the bastard children of the master of the house. Pampered, carefully brought up, they received presents, they learned music, governesses were obtained for them, as in the case of Ginevra, the bastard daughter whom the merchant Datini had by one of his slaves. When Margherite, his wife, mentioned the child, she spoke of her as her own daughter:

> This is the best child in the world. . . . Do not worry about Ginevra [who has a sore throat]. Rest assured that I care for her as if she were my own, and that is just how I think of her. Her head wound is nothing, but I am distressed about her throat.

Moreover, the little Ginevra is asked for in marriage when she is only nine years old, and she receives a dowry of 1,000 florins, more than even the legitimate daughters of great merchants. This practice does not seem to be reserved for daughters: in fifteenth-century Genoa, a young boy named Maurizio receives a dowry of 1,000 liras.[52] Set free—but only after the death of the master—and enriched, slaves or their descendants can even rise to nobility, Italian fashion. We are very far removed here from the bad treatment reserved for African slaves in modern times. But it is true that we only really know about the cases of those who led successful lives.

Thus, slave or free, working children were an undeniable social reality. They obviously constituted a supplementary work force. With some exceptions—too many exceptions, it is true—which constituted aggressions on the part of abusive masters, but which were judged as such, children do not seem to have been maltreated nor introduced too early to the active life. It does not seem as though medieval children were exploited as they would be in the nineteenth century. Let us remember that in France, the first social law concerning child labor, which dates from 1844,[53] brought to light living conditions clearly more difficult than those of the Middle Ages: henceforth, factories and manufacturers could no longer employ children *of less than eight years old*, schedules could not exceed eight hours a day for children from eight to ten years old, and ten hours a day for children from twelve to sixteen years. It is doubtful that medieval children suffered so much in the working world. Today, 73 million children in the world work; that is one out of eight. And children today are not protected by apprenticeship contracts, as they were in the Middle Ages.

EIGHT

Children on the Streets

However, all children were not supervised. If the home constituted the universe of earliest childhood, the street was where, from the age of three or four, children exercised their freedom, sometimes at the expense of public order. In thirteenth- and fourteenth-century Italy, as well as England, there is mention of young "toughs" who attack religious edifices, throwing "stones at the baptistery or the cathedral to damage the sculptures or paintings," as in Parma, or boys characterized as "good-for-nothing, insolent, and idle," for shooting rocks and arrows at the pigeons and crows, playing ball in the church and church square, and breaking stained-glass windows and statues, as at Saint Paul's of London in 1385.[1] It must have been observing these bands of youths that led Italian preachers to assemble small children and make them instrumental in raising moral standards at the end of the Middle Ages. At the time of Savonarole, there are those who, with their stones, chase tramps, hound prostitutes and card or dice players,[2] or even, to the great horror of adults, go after the condemned or the bodies of the tortured.[3] In France, preachers charge bands of children to defend morality: they are seen running after coquettes, crying "*Au hennin! Au hennin!*" thus exposing them to public condemnation.[4] They also spread political songs, as in Paris at the time of the Armagnacs and the Burgundians: "Duke of Burgundy, God keep you happy."[5] Consequently, street children played an undeniable social role. Children found, abandoned, or on charity accompanied funeral processions. Others were coerced into joining religious processions, demonstrations, theatrical pieces of Saint John and May Day, or Christmas dances alongside adults. At the time of penitence, before Easter, when the bells were silent, it was the children who were asked to operate the counter-clocks or wooden hammers during mass and in the street. During major holidays in the year, they went from door to door begging, sometimes aggressively, for food or money, especially on the day of "*aguillaneuf*" (au gui l'an neuf—literally, to the mistletoe new year). At Easter, before the adults, they played at running poultry and rolling eggs, games which were not without religious significance: the egg is the Easter egg, the hen which is caught and made a martyr symbolizing Christ being put to death by the Jews.

In towns as well as in the country, it seems that boys older than seven often spent many hours of the day wandering about away from home, and their parents did not worry about their absence until mealtime. The poet, Froissart, remembers his marvelous escapes, and their unfortunate consequences: "I only had to see my companions pass my house, and I had soon found an excuse for going out to play with them." Punishment followed. But if the little Jean was beaten, it was not for leaving home without permission, it was for his torn clothes:

> I fought with the other children,
> I was beaten and I beat them,
> And I was so furious then
> That often I went home
> With my clothes torn.
> Then I was scolded
> And often I was beaten, but
> A blow on top of that didn't do a thing
> Because, for all of that, I would not restrain myself.[6]

Thus, even though they lived in a rough world, children were not deprived of their freedom, or of pleasures, despite their obligations to help parents with housework. They led the true life of the child. Boys wandered about everywhere. When they were very small, they amused themselves in the courtyard pulling a miniature wooden wagon on wheels, a kitten at their side, while their mother milked the sheep at the door of the farm, as is shown so beautifully in a French manuscript from the fifteenth century. In winter, they made snowballs. In summer, they went swimming in the rivers, and picked cherries or red berries, which shepherds and children delighted in, as we learn from the thirteenth-century encyclopedist, Barthélemy l'Anglais. The children of Domrémy visited the tree of the Ladies, braiding garlands, which they offered to the image of the Virgin hanging there. They sang and danced around the beech tree. The role freedom played in the daily lives of rural sons and daughters must have been very significant, despite the work they were obliged to do for their parents. Thus, in her trial, some witnesses testify that Joan of Arc often went to church when her parents thought she was "at the plow, in the fields, or elsewhere." However, "she never hung about in the streets," as one witness says, in a revealing way.[7]

Accidents

It is hard for us today to understand such freedom, so dangerous for children, in a society which otherwise protected the child and advocated, according to the law at least, attentive supervision of children up to the age of reason, indeed even up to the age of ten. But it was already difficult, even then, for mothers to coordinate paid—or farm—work and family. And it might also have been the value of learning the hard way, the important experience of taking one's knocks, that accounts for this familial behavior. Evidence of overprotection disappears after the early years, at least for boys, because little girls, occupied with domestic tasks, more often stayed inside the house. Actually, animals represented a primary danger for these children who played in the streets everyday. Adults were aware of this: a formulary from fourteenth-century English baptism asks "that this child be protected from water, from fire, from the feet of horses, and the teeth of dogs."[8] The pig escaped from its pen who bites a child, the donkey who gives a deadly kick, all these animals, and their masters, were often judged and condemned, the masters to paying a fine, the animal to being killed for having killed or wounded a child. Thus, in the fourteenth and fifteenth centuries, records from court proceedings and stories mention the costs of execution, sometimes for a donkey, sometimes for three small pigs guilty of such crimes. Legal sources and miracle accounts show that the streets of big cities were just as dangerous then as they are today and that accidents involving children certainly took place. In London, children hauled themselves up onto the piles of tree trunks stacked and waiting for carpenters, or did acrobatics on the great bridge—and were killed.[9] Little girls played while they drew water from the river or the stream running through their town or their village—and fell in. The town was not safe: wells and cellars were the principle places of high risk. A child could slide under the wheels of a wagon. Town houses, with many stories, were potentially dangerous. Children played on the wooden balconies, as in Italy, and fell from high up. Even those who sat patiently waiting on their doorsteps were not safe from the kick of a wooden shoe or a malevolent stranger. In the country, the open hearths led to often serious burns, the rivers and ponds to drowning, no doubt the most common accident for children, with their many falls. As is the case today, parents with large families could not manage to maintain constant supervision. For all that, accidents did not mean that parents were being irresponsible in bringing up their children.

Other children, in another category altogether and left to their own devices, lived on the streets. Despite charitable organizations, which were mostly urban, there were children who existed on the margins of medieval society. Poverty increased in the fourteenth and fifteenth centuries. To consider an example which no doubt applies generally, in Lyons, 40 percent of the inhabitants lived under precarious conditions, and 10 percent of the poor survived on charity alone. In 1420, it upset the Paris bourgeoisie to see the mothers of families, "poor creatures," lining up at the bakery doors while their children were dying of hunger at home. Among the poor, a fringe element were reduced to becoming vagabonds and beggars. In order to survive, their children behaved as predators. Even then, the whole problem of childhood delinquency already existed.

Little Thieves

Stealing was another way of earning money. And not the easiest way, either. Merchants who suspected theft had quick hands: in 1324, an English child, five years old, taken to stealing wool by hiding it in his hat, died from being slapped too violently by an angry merchant.[10] Authorities did not hesitate to arrest children recognized to be little thieves. And what happened to them then? In the fourteenth and fifteenth centuries, they were put in prisons and flogged, as, for example, were three "young children" of Châlon who had stolen money[11] or a little "cutter of purses," nine years old, practicing his talents in the halls of Paris: this is the pickpocket, a specialty of little boys with lightening hands and quick feet; others specialized in stripping birdlimed tree trunks.[12] The reaction of society to these little crimes was not, generally, excessive. In the mid-thirteenth century, the lawyer, Philippe de Beaumanoir advocated taking into account both the nature of the offense and the age of the offender: "When a child who is underage commits a crime, one must consider the way the event took place and the child's discretion according to his age." The merchant who punishes the urchin to the point of hurting him is the one who gets arrested and condemned, not the child. Before the age of seven, indeed even up to the age of ten, children were not considered responsible for their actions. In the thirteenth century, some educators even give advice regarding cases in which the child has stolen something for the first time. Berthold de Ratisbonne recommends:

> If a child learns to steal for the first time, if he takes or steals one thing or another, correct him immediately with a switch, and make him return what he has stolen to the place he got it; this is the only way to keep him from getting into the habit of pilfering and stealing.[13]

Thus, in the eyes of medieval parents, the first theft was not a catastrophe. No doubt the well-read pedagogues remembered the *Confessions* of Saint Augustine, who himself stole pears in his youth, a theft committed at night in the company of a band of young urchins.[14] Artists testify to this in their own way, and with a certain amount of indulgence, as they enjoyed illustrating the season of summer with the theme of little boys climbing trees to steal cherries, to the great vexation of peasants. This relative equanimity was not limited to petty crimes. Thus, we find hardly one child or adolescent criminal mentioned in the vast body of requests for pardons addressed to the king of France by those condemned by common law. The courts were lenient toward the young. With regard to the last centuries of the Middle Ages, Claude Gauvard even speaks of a "total and systematic clemency" on the part of judges toward children.[15] As far as the law was concerned, age at this early stage of life was always a mitigating circumstance.

Beggars and Guides for the Blind

Some more resourceful youths applied themselves very early to eking out a living at less risk by serving as guides to the blind and accompanying them on their begging rounds. A theatrical "play" from the thirteenth century, *The Boy and the Blind Man*, portrays one of them swindling the unfortunate invalid—who takes him on as valet—with impunity, the boy occupying himself by protecting the blind man from obstacles and begging for him at the doors of wealthy residences. This "play" is no doubt based on a social reality, that of young people without families, runaways perhaps, clever certainly, who knew "so well [how to] make faces, act poor, and play the kitchen boy/That those who not giving something would be despised."[16]

The historical reality is harsher still. The interrogation of a blind man from the *Hôpital des Quinze-Vingts*, founded in Paris in the thirteenth century, mentions the hardships of the "little boy" who helped him in his begging. The text recounts how the child was badly treated by passers-by, who made his begging bowl fall by hitting his arm or filled it with mud, who threw lead tokens to him as they passed, or even stones, who stole the very rock upon which he sat to beg.[17] At the end of the Middle Ages, the young beggar's fate is not rosy, confronting a society which does not always show enough respect and Christian charity toward the poor, or what is more, the invalid and the sick. Young guides to the blind are mentioned quite often in miracles accounts, but it is generally a matter of the sons or daughters of the sick, accompanying them from sanctuary to sanctuary, following an endless pilgrimage. It must not have been uncommon to spend one's youth on the road in this way. Blind youths, guided by a dog trained to carry the begging bowl in its mouth, were also painted by artists in the books of hours* used by the laity. This was a matter of inspiring the noble readers of these books to be compassionate and charitable. Indeed, begging constituted one way of earning a living for a child, in a manner of speaking. In the medieval images, we observe that all beggars responsible for families put their children in front of them: in a world where suspicion of the poor had become the rule, childhood, pure, innocent, unfortunate, still brought in money. A child who was poor and sick evoked twice the pity of passers-by. Indeed, it was believed that the prayers of the poor and of children were the most effective, God having most pity on them and listening to them most willingly.

Child Martyrs

Adult beggars understood this new situation very well. They did not hesitate to "kidnap" very young children and mutilate them in order to make them more pitiable in the eyes of passers-by. In 1440 and 1449, the bourgeoisie of Paris evoke these "caimans, thieves, and murderers" who confessed to having lifted children "from the open-air market," and "as for one of them, put out his eyes, another, cut off his legs, others, their feet."[18] In Tuscany, the doctor, Barberino, also mentions beggars who steal children to cripple them. Other abductions were carried out for the purpose of obtaining a ransom. In 1449, the bourgeoisie of Paris explain that child-snatchers choose newborns, not yet baptized. Their parents, convinced that an unbaptized child will never be admitted into paradise, are more willing to pay. Child thieves also kidnapped street urchins they found walking alone, "along village paths or elsewhere." This is exactly the misfortune that befalls a Florentine boy, about ten years old, by the name of Donato Velluti, in the first half of the fourteenth century.[19] Tricked by one man, carried off by ransomers, he is only saved thanks to the presence of mind of an innkeeper who recognizes him to be a son of a good family, and, astonished to see him in the company of bandits, calls the guard. This is undoubtedly the way thieves recruited the youths they then mutilated or blinded in order to win the pity of passers-by. The abduction of children is one of the great medieval terrors. Child abductions—about forty of them, if we are to believe his court proceedings—were also blamed, rightly or wrongly, on the famous Gilles de Rais. But for a different end: debauchery.

Prostitution and Pedophilia

Other children were particularly maltreated: there is no lack of texts describing their fate. These were the young prostitutes put to work by their mothers, a parent, or a neighbor.[20] Often they were under the age of ten, but pimping more often involved girls from ten to fourteen years old.[21] In the thirteenth century, Berthold de Ratisbonne notes with alarm the existence of child thieves and debauched youths, "because there are many of them who begin very early. In truth, I have been told of a young girl of eight years who has already disappeared with a gentleman."[22] A madam accused of having prostituted her young servant defends herself by saying that after the age of thirteen, she had found her "putting her fingers into her nature . . . to enlarge it,"[23] an ambiguous defense, suggesting that the girl was licentious and naturally immoral. But the origin of their debauchery is first and foremost, rape by an employer, a farmhand, or by a nobleman: in the fifteenth century, a Catalan knight goes to court for having raped children. After this act, dishonored, girls sometimes have no other recourse than the public house. In general, they are servants, orphans, and adolescents: the adolescent is at a high-risk age, especially when she is growing up without the protection of a family. We know that for the repentant prostitutes of Avignon, one out of three began working at the oldest trade in the world before celebrating their fifteenth birthday.[24] If mother madams existed, in general, their children escaped their profession. In the fourteenth century, municipalities took charge of the children of "little girls," if the latter had no means of feeding them. Boys, too, did not escape sexual violence, however short-lived. Gilles de Rais is accused of appreciating them too much—they died of it.

Little martyrs, gypsy children deliberately mutilated to win more pity from passers-by, prostitutes hardly having reached puberty: all these cases constituted the hidden side of medieval childhood. They do not appear in the images: the phenomenon was too shocking. Medieval society claimed to be horrified by their fate, as we see in the newspaper commentaries of the Paris bourgeoisie. The unfortunate child attracted pity and the swindler profited from this fact: paradoxically, abuse derived in part from the extent to which children were valued.

Vagrant Families

Beginning from the fourteenth century, poverty established itself in the towns. A population already just getting by on inadequate income dropped below the poverty line. These impoverished were called the "nihil habens": those who had nothing. For all that, they were not completely without refuge, and some families experienced ups and downs; their children did not all become beggars. Those who lost the roofs over their heads became itinerants, indeed even pilgrims. By the fifteenth century, whole families took to the road in this way, each night finding a new place to stay, a hospital or monastery. If it is difficult to estimate the size of this homeless population, medieval art does provide some striking images of this way of life. Beggars burdened with young children fashion for themselves make-shift baby-carriers in the form of baskets or backpacks; children travel with their parents, some on foot, some on the shoulders of their father or mother, according to their age. They are never alone. They beg for alms as a family, and, if we can believe the images, this procedure is highly effective: it is always to the children that the first piece of bread or the first coin is given. Despite their poverty, these children no doubt suffer only from cold, and sometimes, hunger, but not from being abandoned. This continues until the end of the Middle Ages, little pilgrims accompanying their parents, semi-professional vagabonds taking begging to its limits. Bearing the signs of their vocation, shells and the pilgrim's staff—their walking stick—a miniature version of their parents', they successfully extend their begging bowls at the entrances of castles or wealthy town houses. Indeed, in the last centuries of the Middle Ages, noble women and the bourgeoisie are taught to practice systematic charity, giving alms to the first poor person they encountered along the way in the morning and going to mass, especially to a poor father with children or, as Raymond Lulle explains, to "every poor woman holding a poor child in her arms," the living image of the Virgin with Child.

But certain parents resolved not to beg. Thus, as the Middle Ages progressed, charitable institutions became responsible for providing minimal subsistence for them. Thus, in Florence, the *Buinomini*, the "good men," made home deliveries of blankets and baby's wraps to poor women who had just given birth, as well as food, and perhaps especially, moral comfort. They distributed other things as well, bread, wine, and even clothes—surely the most expensive budget item of everyday life. Finally, as in fifteenth-century Sienna, the poor—and in the first rows, we always see starving children, as in the La Scala hospital frescoes—found "handouts" of bread at urban hospitals. And, as we know from written sources, there were parents who abandoned their children, not only at birth, but even between the ages of five and eight years old. This was not considered shocking, as long as it was done because of poverty, in front of the church or near a hospital. In Florence, it was one of the responsibilities of the Hospital of the Innocents to collect the "discarded," or abandoned, children. The same institutions made an effort to place orphans in apprenticeships, just as they did for abandoned children. That is how three little girls were placed with three mistresses who would teach them silk working.[25] Finally, still in Florence, as in many other towns, there was a community chest to provide endowments for poor young women.

Without Family

Abandoned children found a kind reception in special hospitals, which constituted the oldest form of child protection.[26] However, their life expectancy was reduced; nearly 40 percent died before the age of six months to one year, but not because of poor treatment. Often they could not tolerate their early transport to the wet nurse in difficult climatic conditions, lying with many others in a basket suspended from a shoulder yoke, as we see in pictures. Weakened by communal life, which made them more susceptible to epidemics, they also suffered from early weaning or a change in nurses. At seven years old, they came back to the hospital where, in addition to necessary medical care, they received food and clothes, religious, academic, and then professional training, to finally be given a dowry and married. If the first hospitals for abandoned children, founded as early as the eighth century, were hardly numerous, they multiplied in the twelfth and thirteenth centuries, principally under the aegis of the order of Saint-Esprit which devoted itself to their survival. They existed throughout, in France, Italy, Germany, and Poland. At the end of the Middle Ages, municipalities linked efforts with charitable institutions to take in little abandoned children whose numbers grew, not only in relation to the difficulty of the times, but also with the improved conditions for their reception. The temptation of parents under duress to give up their children became too strong. To avoid increased abandonment, the statutes of these establishments stipulated that all the "discarded" children, as they called them in Italy, could not be taken in. The situation became even worse during great catastrophes, plagues, epidemics, or famines, which turned out into the streets hordes of abandoned children, or, as was more often the case, children left without resources following the death of their parents. In the fifteenth century, the Paris bourgeoisie lament:

> And on the dung heaps around Paris, can't you find ten, twenty, or thirty children, sons and daughters, who died there of hunger or of cold, and was there ever so hard a heart which, by night, heard them cry "Alas, I am dying of hunger!" and felt no great pity for them.[27]

In the same period, urban society also sporadically experimented with taking children away from beggar parents, in conjunction with an automatic placement for them, as in Reims in 1454.[28] At the beginning of modern times, in Strasbourg, there was an attempt to separate beggar children from their parents to place them in apprenticeships, in order to break the vicious circle of poverty. The motivations for this communal intervention were probably benevolent, but as a consequence, children lost their legitimate families, with which they were not necessarily unhappy. Society incidentally stumbled over the fact that, in order to be operational, the apprenticeship system needed a supervisory authority which could pay for the professional training of these children; but no one wanted that responsibility.[29] These lost children were a minority. For another minority, the privileged, the children of the castle, the situation was entirely different.

NINE

The Child in the Castle

It is surely the noble childhood which we know best: most of the sources emanate from this social class. As with the peasants, large families are the rule. However, it is difficult to estimate the child population living in the castle. Even if nobility represented only a tiny fraction of the population, the number of castles built between the twelfth and fifteenth century is, nevertheless, very large. The ruins remaining today attest to at least thirty thousand of them. Consequently, many children lived there, even if it is necessary to subtract from this number those who, because of their birth rank in relation to their brothers, were entrusted to monasteries. Furthermore, young nobles were not the only ones to live at the castles. As in the towns, apprentices were there to learn trades, indeed even in the hopes of finding a career in the stable, the wine cellar, or the kitchen. The children of artisans personally employed by the lord apparently mixed with the children of nobility, and sometimes renounced the manual trades of their father to become famous troubadours, for instance, as did Bernard de Ventadour, the son of a supplier for the castle of Ventadour in the twelfth century. The castle was a true melting pot, where nobility and non-nobility lived together, and where the sons and daughters of the lord could benefit by learning how to behave toward those representing other social classes.

Kitchen Children

Indeed, a castle constituted a community of inhabitants with very diverse backgrounds and of all ages. It was a long-standing draw for tradesmen: blacksmiths to repair weapons and shoe horses, servants to take care of rooms, wash the linens, make clothes, and feed the masters and those in their service. This last budget item sometimes required the employment of numerous personnel, including young boys. The texts call them the "kitchen children" or even the *"galopins,"* "ragamuffins." Their job was to clean the fish and the poultry, to pluck them, and to turn the spit, a tiring, even painful, activity. The illuminators show us these children grimacing as they turn away, protecting their faces with a raised hand, or, if the head cook is kind, with a wooden platter he has lent them to use as a shield against the flames. In the kitchen, they performed "*menus services*," "small services," as the medieval texts say, which were, no doubt, not all that small: the term simply means that it was not a matter of being responsible for important tasks. The kitchen children were also in charge of the trash and sweeping up. Their long workdays did not inhibit them from being as unruly as all other children their age. They quarreled, bickered, and the cook, seated in a chair like a schoolmaster, was obliged to drive them out.[1] "The chef, an old text tells us, must have in his hand a big wooden soup ladle . . . to chase the children out of the kitchen, to make them do their work, and to hit them on the head, if need be."

Even in the area of entertainment, we find the youngest inhabitants of the castle at work. Children could be engaged as musicians, as we see in the princely accounts. On occasion, they were paid; in the records of King René d'Anjou, for December 1479, we read of "five little girls who came to sing Noël."[2] Children also functioned as "actors" during the great "interludes" performed at the feasts of high nobility. In his cookbook, Jehan Chiquart, the head chef for the Savoie dukes in the fifteenth century, noted one of these mid-meal diversions in which the children played a part. Installed in a miniature castle, the little musicians were thus presented to the dining hall to entertain the noble guests. These children were not necessarily of low birth: they must have already known how to play music! In the margins of the books of hours owned by fourteenth-century noblewomen, we also see frolicking children dressed up as "fools," all their little bells jingling, no doubt to illustrate the medieval proverb, "one must be wary of the fool and the child."

Stable Boys and Little Pages

Did these same kitchen children take care of the horses? The term, "*galopin*," which designated the former, could be understood to include the latter: in the iconography of the mages, Galopin is, indeed, the name of the horseback rider. Whatever the case, the care of the horses is one of the tasks belonging to castle children. The "*galopins*" clean the stable, the pages take care of the animals. In the fourteenth-century German manuscript, it is a beautiful blond child in a long dress, an indication of his youthfulness, who holds his lord's horse by the reins and takes pleasure in petting the noble animal's nose to calm him when he snorts and stamps the ground. At tournaments as in wars, the page was responsible for the horse, indeed even for the master himself. At the end of the fifteenth century, when knights in tournaments wore such heavy and impenetrable armor that they had difficulty seeing or directing their mounts, it was the oldest pages, the riders, who led the galloping beasts by the reins into combat with the adversary.

Becoming an excellent rider was just as necessary as becoming a good driver is today. Even more so, perhaps: during military confrontations, excellent horsemanship was a factor in survival. Pages were also trained in equitation, not only through hunts, but also through actual horse races, which are first mentioned in the eleventh century in Brittany. The pages were the jockeys, on whom, at the end of the fifteenth century, the lords did not hesitate to bet money. Philippe de Vigneulles recalls with amusement this scene which he personally observed in his town of Metz:

> The day of Saint Clement, the duke of Siffort undertook to race his horses once again, with a page, against the lord Nicolle Dex (who had already raced the previous year on the same day); and bet the sum of twenty-one gold crowns on this race. But, by ill-luck, the duke's page let himself fall to the ground.[3]

The Kennel Boys

In the kennels, other children did their apprenticeships as *"valets de chien,"* "dog servants." This was an occupation long reserved for children. In Carolingian times, the adolescent was considered an accomplished "bachelor"—the term is still used today, but to mark the end of secondary studies!—when they knew how to give the quarry to the hounds. The young boy's job, which we sometimes see him performing in the illuminations or tapestries, is described in detail by the fourteenth-century master of the hunt, Gaston Phébus. It was required

> in the first place . . . for him to learn and to give in writing all the names of the dogs and the bitches of the kennel, until the child knows them by coat and by name; next, I want him to learn to clean all the dog dirt from the kennels each morning; next, I want him to learn to put fresh water into the dogs' drinking bowl two times a day, morning and night. . . . Next, I want him to learn to rearrange the bedding where the dogs lie, every three days, without turning it upside down; next, I want him to learn to clean the kennel well and empty it out once a week, including the bedding, and to put down new bedding, clean and white, a good deal of it, and very thick.[4]

This apprenticeship, which began with lessons, involved little boys. According to Gaston Phébus, it was a matter of taking on a child at the age of reason and placing him under the firm hand of a "good master" with a taste and a love for dogs (and for children, one would hope), even if he must also "beat him when he disobeys in order to teach him and to keep him from failing":

> Whether you be a great or minor lord, if you want to have a man instructed so that he will become a good huntsman, choose, first of all, a child of seven years old at the most, and, even though men would rebuke me for putting so young a child to work with the dogs, I would answer that natural talents are altered and diminished with time; because we cannot ignore the fact that a seven-year-old child today knows more about whatever he likes or whatever he learns than a twelve-year-old child knew in my time. That is why I want to put him to work so young, because a craft requires a man's entire lifetime to be perfected. That is why it is said, "what one learns in his youth, he retains in his old age."[5]

Thus, being very young is, in general, considered reason enough to exempt children from work, and the author of the *Book of the Hunt* places himself in a precarious position here with regard to his contemporaries who "would rebuke [him] for putting so young a child to work with the dogs," according to his own words. Indeed, at the end of the thirteenth century, Philippe de Novare advises parents not to put children to work before the age of twelve, not even "to the work of chivalry." But working at the age of seven, which was called the "age of reason," was not out of the question. It was also the age at which young nobles themselves, still very small ("babies" as they were called in one English book of comportment written for them in about 1475), had to leave their families to go far away to learn to serve in the court and the military. Because, according to the educators, "of all occupations most suitably begun in early childhood, these are the two highest and most honorable in the eyes of God and the times: the clergy and chivalry."

The Band of Young Nobles

Within the castle walls, however, the majority of children were nobles. These were sons of the lord, and youths invited there by the lord, who saw to their upbringing for several years. Indeed, the castles of great noblemen were often overrun by pages, who came there to finish their chivalric training. It was around 1115, when William Marshall was about eleven or twelve years old, that he left his family home to become "pure" at his uncle's. Taken in by an uncle, often chosen from the maternal branch of the family, or by a lord who was friends with his father and, preferably, more powerful than him, the young noble assumed multiple responsibilities. Between seven and ten years old, he was educated by observing gestures and manners, learning "*contenances*" or comportment, especially at the table. At about ten years old, he left to train at another castle. At the age of sixteen or seventeen, he became a horseman. Thus, he reached the summit of his career. At the end of the Middle Ages, very few young nobles finally became armed knights. Their daily life was tiring, but agreeable. Those of them who resided with the highest nobility wore the bright "*mi-parties*"* livery of their lord and enlivened the castle with appropriate youthful spirit. They learned to play the trumpet. They played and trained in the courtyard. Their childhood was not stolen from them, even if they no longer lived with their families and had to attend to certain duties. To carry their lord's sword or helmet, take care of his arms, groom his horse and hold it by the reins, to remain standing still and observant during the lower court and council sessions. . . . As adolescents, they also served the noblewomen. In illuminations or tapestries from the end of the Middle Ages, we see them occupied with various little tasks: working the bellows on the organ for the lord's wife, holding up her short train so it would not be soiled by touching the ground. Indeed, ladies seemed to take pleasure in going to town with an entourage of small pages, doing the shopping with a page to hold the wicker basket for all her little items or attending mass with a small follower to carry her rosary beads and book of hours.

Military Training

But these are the occupations of pages in urban castles in the late Middle Ages, a period when the art of living tends to overshadow the art of war. One part of the "work day" of the future knight involved outside activity, both an obligation and a pleasure. A pleasure, as we see in the thirteenth-century *Roman de Silence*, which portrays a young girl disguised as a boy since her earliest days. The male child loved to "be exposed to wind and to sun . . . to walk in the forest, to throw darts, draw arrows, hunt with a bow."[6] In the romance of the *Enfances Vivien*, the young hero is eight years old when he asks for a horse and dogs. In the fourteenth century, Jean de Berry is not yet twelve when he is fully equipped and outfitted to do what he wants. Hunting, notably with falcons, was not reserved for boys. Children of both sexes kept this animal as a favorite companion, learning to feed it and to carry it on their wrists. The link which united man or child to falcon was so strong that in the fourteenth and fifteenth centuries in Forez, the first name of Falcon was given to boys, and to girls as well, in the feminine! An obligation: it was also a matter of physical training for children and adolescents. In the twelfth century, the military training of young Tristan consisted of learning "to be very agile with his hands and his legs: to throw stones, to run and jump, to fight with skill, to throw the javelin with force, like a valiant warrior." Children were required to learn agility through hunting, and strength and endurance through wearing small suits of armor, evidently meant for children under ten years old. One of these suits still survives, that of Charles VI. It only measures seventy centimeters in height. These various physical exercises were considered good for health. Sweat, says Raymond Lulle, rids children of "bad humors" and is appropriate to the role young nobles are to play. Exercise, according to Giles of Rome, "strengthens," "toughens," and "makes supple" the limbs; it keeps the body from becoming "heavy" and "sluggish." Evidently, the prototype of fat, clumsy little boys was not a model for medieval nobility, which dreamed of lively, combative, if not to say aggressive, youngsters. To this end, children of the castle were encouraged to engage in competitions, and the adults carefully observed their progress.

Included in the program of physical exercise were walks, races, wrestling, throwing weights—from simple stones to javelins, and the art of hand-to-hand combat. The young were trained in fencing, at first with the help of wooden swords, later, with smaller versions of metal swords. These two kinds of children's weapons have been unearthed by archaeological digs. Archery was an essential discipline in a noble education. It was learned young, by boys six to eight years old. Many texts mention little bows which children used to shoot birds, be it the very young, shooting cherry pits, or those a bit older shooting wooden arrows. But at ten years old, a child could use a lethal arrow.[7] Many illuminators portray this exercise, at once military and sporting, as practiced by adolescents. They practiced in the castle garden, under the critical eye of grown men. A wooden target mounted on a large mound of earth or straw lowered the risk of accidents from stray arrows. If we are to believe the archaeological digs of

Charavines, in the Isère, there might even have been cross-bows for children in the eleventh century. In any case, we see an example of them from the sixteenth century in a Flemish engraving of Stradanus. In adolescence, and then in the first stages of adulthood, this training continued. In Italian cities, it was even the special privilege of youth.[8]

Gymnastics seem to have been practiced regularly by young noblemen. They practiced doing headstands, as well as contortions to learn to free themselves of straps binding their wrists behind their backs, no doubt as a safeguard against being taken prisoner someday. They also learned to withstand cold and pain, and a number of boys' games consisted of hitting themselves, sometimes on the nose—this was "*la nasarde*"—sometimes on the backside, with the help of an iron shovel! Indeed, this was all part of the training for toughening the body which, even at the end of the fifteenth century, educators recommended to young nobility. In the thirteenth century, Raymond Lulle and Giles of Rome advised parents to dress their children lightly in winter in order to toughen them. In the fifteenth century, Jean de Bueil, the author of *Jouvencel*,[9] a didactic romance intended for young nobles, as its title suggests, reminds them that it is necessary to "avoid the pleasures of the body, such as too much drinking, too much eating, and too much sleep." He advises the future knight to fast, and "to wear the harness night and day," to train himself to sleep on the bare ground and without heat, as he would have to do in the country. He praises the science of camouflage and clever warrior tactics, worthy of the Sioux: the young must learn to crawl on their stomachs to hide themselves, erase their footprints, cover the fences of neighbors, sawed in advance, with earth or wax, "keep their horses from crying out, "attack at nightfall so that the "*fourragères*" will not hear them, cover their "helmets [with leaves] so that they do not gleam at all," and not let the enemy discover them too soon. Courage itself, which does not come naturally, had to be carefully cultivated: to learn to keep one's head, to be ashamed of cowardice and idleness, were part of the training.

Equitation

A horse was a living weapon, it might be said. This was surely the way horses were introduced to children. Thus, to learn to ride a horse was a vital necessity, and instruction began very early, as with the young Tristan who, in the twelfth century, left his nurse the day he could ride. In the illuminations, we see children whose feet barely reach below the saddle. Sayings confirm that this precocious training was common: "the one who has not learned to ride young will never ride well," says the thirteenth-century educator, Philippe de Novare. Or again, "Whoever stays at school, never riding a horse, until they are twelve years old, is no longer good for anything but the clergy." Education manuals give advice on how to help young horses and young children get used to each other: the young horse is carefully fettered in its stall, the child, perched on its back, immobile, speaks to it and calms it with caresses until the animal gets used to the child's weight and presence. Afterwards, the child learns actual equitation.

Images show us how, in order to go along on a hunt, the underage child rides behind his father, holding onto the high cantle of the saddle, while the older brother rides on a pretty young horse wearing a harness decorated with bells. As an adolescent, one practiced riding bareback in the castle courtyard. And finally, one practiced guiding the horse with just one hand, the other one serving to carry the falcon, the shield, or the lance. But jousting was not initially learned on horseback: for reasons of safety, this exercise was first practiced on foot. Boys rushed at a makeshift lance, made out of cane or millet stalks, or aimed at a target hung on a post. After that, they practiced on a pommel horse on wheels, which other boys pulled, running, toward the target, a horseshoe hung on a pivoting arm, from the other end of which hung a sack of bran or sand meant to hit them soundly on the back if they did not go fast enough. It was only when the young mastered both the science of equitation and the art of taking aim that they combined the two activities.

War Games

With adolescence, military training became more serious. Educators advised parents to "apply their children to war" by entrusting them to the military captain of the castle, "without giving them rank or servants." It was necessary for them to learn to obey and to be self-sufficient. Undoubtedly, this rough apprenticeship constituted a serious break with the comfort of the family castle. Furthermore, a share of the military work fell to the young, and it was decidedly not the most gratifying share. Thus, the watch was willingly entrusted to "young children," who sometimes did not perform it very seriously.[10] The term is misleading. In reality, a minimum age of fourteen years was required for those standing watch. The fifteenth-century *Jouvencel* explains that the task of checking the ditches to make sure no enemies were hiding in them was assigned to pages (but also to women and dogs). We also learn from legal sources that other "young children" could have been engaged as spies. This was the case in 1432, in Châlon. When they were caught, it was considered adequate punishment to whip them with a birch-rod and chase them off (while their adult counterparts would have been hung), since it was well known that they were not responsible for their actions in times of war, anymore than in times of peace.

Among the high nobility, children could be introduced to the matters of war at a very young age. In the twelfth century, the life of William Marshall reminds us that a young noble serves as a good hostage on occasion, handed over by his own father to an enemy king.[11] Even if the innocence of childhood nearly always disarmed the warrior, and if, as in this case, the latter brought the child into his tent to play games of skill with him using blades of grass, the trauma—or the pride—of this memory no doubt stayed with the little hostage a long time. The enemy also made a show of leading him to the gallows and even of transforming him into a missile for the catapult! It was especially important for an adolescent to be put to the test, even in times of peace. Hunting was only the first exercise in a child's training. He then had to put into practice all he had been taught. In the twelfth century, for his first field experience, the father of the future

Saint Hugues of Grenoble made his son go pillage the neighboring residences in order to toughen him. This was, no doubt, a common enough practice among nobility, and it is mentioned in the *Jouvencel* as well. The adolescent gets sent to steal no more and no less than the neighbor's livestock! The goal of the operation was to accustom the young noble to moving about at night, silently and secretly. If he succeeded in surprising the adversary's watch—an adversary who could do nothing about it—without being taken, he was declared in some way ready for service. That is how the young noble in the romance finds himself charged with stealing the goats from the neighboring castle, and he does not hesitate to steal the castle captain's washing, and put holes in the lining of his *"jacque,"* a short military doublet. He then steals the horses, and then the captain's cow, but returns it to him, all the same, when he asks, because the cow provides milk for his son. All this seems permissible, even encouraged, by the family circle and the willing victims, and today, seems very petty, but "the one who wishes to attain good results must not begin by undertaking too much." The author of the *Jouvencel* concludes with this proverb. These "first victories" of the future knight, in reality, mark the beginning of a career which he will have to follow up with jousts and tournaments, and crown some day on the first of May—the month of youth and chivalry—by the being dubbed. Dubbing was still a very important practice among nobility in the thirteenth century, although later, it tends to fall out of use or only takes place when a noble comes of age at twenty-one, as in royal circles. In the fourteenth and fifteenth centuries, the highest nobility were no longer automatically dubbed, even though children of four years old, such as Philippe de Bourgogne, could be, and Jean de Berry almost was, at eleven years old, in the mid-fourteenth century.

Daily Life at the Castle

Given all this, to live at the castle did not mean living in comfort: most castles were not at all comfortable. In royal residences, on the other hand, for a child like the future duke of Berry, for example,[12] life was extraordinarily luxurious. Twice a year, at All Saints Day and at Easter, the bedrooms were redecorated, at Easter, going from red to green, the color of spring, and from lawn to "daisies." Even the chairs in children's rooms were redone at these two times of the year. For important ceremonies, like Jean de Berry's dubbing, the decor of the young boy's room was changed. The regular curtains were put away, and the room decorated over again in fabrics of symbolic colors: black for penitence and red for glory. Moreover, at princely castles, an unusual piece of furniture testifies to the attention given to royal children's welfare: for the very small, the accounts mention cradles, a rare commodity among rural folk. The little princes often owned two types, one for sleeping in, and one, said to be *"de parement,"* or ceremonial, decorated with coats of arms, for presenting them at court. In some instances, the cradle was covered with ermine, as much to keep the child warm as to show the power of his family, or covered with mosquito netting. When he was older, the young prince found his wardrobe furnished with *"chaises à peigner"* and *"chaises nécessaires,"* or commodes, very comfortably made: they were lined with felt and covered in leather or cloth. Boxes with sugar-covered almonds were left in the little prince's apartment, and "beribboned bells," to play with, for music, or to call the servants. The wardrobes of princely children were unusually rich and varied. New clothes were provided for all the important holidays of the year, Christmas, Easter, Ascension, Pentecost, "Mid-August," Saint Michael's Day, and All Saints Day, and costumes were given to them for the May festival, when all young nobles adorned themselves in green to imitate the leaves. On this occasion, the dress of young Jean, the future duke of Berry, was not only green, it was "foliated" with ivy leaves.[15] If these little gentlemen needed shoes, they were there for the taking. The accounts mention one day's delivery of forty pairs of new shoes to Jean, who was then fifteen years old! On most days, the young prince's companions were all dressed like him, to better teach them to operate as a single unit with their young lord and to make them understand that, later on, on the battlefield, they would have to defend him and help one another.

But this was a way of life completely out of the ordinary. In general, the average castle was designed for defense or war rather than domestic comfort, and, even at the end of the Middle Ages, the atmosphere was more like that of a permanent encampment than an opulent, well-furnished residence. Comfort was more often reserved for the sons and daughters of the bourgeoisie. However, men of war, accompanied by their families, were always trying to find an agreeable living space within the defensive structure of cold, naked stone. Already in the times of wooden castles, women and children had an area especially designated for them. In the twelfth century, Lambert d'Ardres mentions how, in his keep, the large master bedroom was situated between another room for the children and nursemaid, and a private toilet, heated morning and night: that was where sick children stayed and infants were nursed.

The Use of Time

The young noble's day began early. The "long morning," what today we would call "sleeping in," was officially deemed ill advised for them. That would be proof of a "branch" of the sin of sloth, which was then called "carnality." At no later than about seven a.m., the child was awakened and required to say his hours, that is, his prayers. This might have been his mother's responsibility. Indeed, Christine de Pizan suggests that the latter, even if she is of high nobility, visit her children in their chamber, when they are getting up as well as when they are going to bed.[14] The child then dressed and washed his face and hands before going to mass. He was then allowed to finally eat his breakfast, as is explained, not without some humor, in an English book of comportment from the fifteenth century:

> Rise from your bed when it is time, make the sign of the cross on your forehead and your breast, wash your hands and face, comb your hair and ask God's grace that He may aid you in all your tasks; then go to mass and ask forgiveness for all your transgressions. Say hello politely to anyone you meet along the way. That done, break the fast with good food and

drink, but before eating, make the sign of the cross on your mouth; your diet will only be improved by it. Then say grace (that will only require a very little amount of time) and thank the Lord Jesus for your food and your drink.[15]

But this meal was only granted him with a certain amount of reluctance. Nobility did not make a practice of it at all. It is difficult, however, to resist the cries of famished youth. And if some grumpy educator, like Raymond Lulle in the thirteenth century, is upset by their bad manners and their inability to endure hunger when they wake up, if Aldebrandin of Sienna advocates giving them only bread in the morning, and refusing them all "*lècherie*," that is, cake, and especially pâtés, tortes, flans, and fruit, which tells us a good deal about the tastes of children, mothers no doubt satisfied their children's desires despite these prohibitions. The same was not true for adolescents, notably, for adolescent girls, who required closer supervision. In the fifteenth century, the great nobles, worried about raising their descendants in a suitable fashion, asked doctors to come up with "health diets," or standard menus proposed to the cooks responsible for feeding the lord's progeny. One text, the only one of its kind on the subject, gives information on the meal schedule and table manners of the children, at least seven years old, who live at the castle of the duke of Croy: soups and stews, tender, young meats, fish carefully prepared to avoid accidents, cheese and fruit, wine cut with water hygienically boiled, etc.[16] The day, punctuated by three meals for the very young, and only two for others, was then filled with various activities, play, study, sports or military exercises, some of which the two sexes shared, others of which were designated for one sex or the other.

At the age of five or six, children were entrusted to a private tutor who introduced to them the letters of the alphabets, primers, and then books, in French, beginning from the thirteenth century. A few hours of lessons and activities in keeping with being warriors then took up the boys' days. They built castles out of boughs, like Aelred de Rievaulx and his companions in the twelfth-century courtyard of the Scottish king.[17] They had wooden swords and attended marionettes shows of battles—no doubt based on the chansons de geste—as we see in an English manuscript from the fourteenth century. If their father was often away, their mother willingly remained at home, and Christine de Pizan does not fail to recommend that she have her children brought to her often, to check "their manners and words and deeds" for herself, undoubtedly at the end of the day. If adults at that time liked to go to bed late, after various festivities, educators like Aldebrandin of Sienna advised against having children stay up too long. They were put to bed before the adults, after reciting their prayers for the dead and in honor of their guardian angel, so that they did not risk dying suddenly— the worst death—during the night.

Young Girls and Little Boys

We encounter fewer girls than young men in the large medieval castle, no doubt. However, young men left their families to go into service, while girls stayed at their father's castle and grew up under their mother's supervision. Young girls were hardly the favorite subjects of artists, who systematically gave preference to boys. There are no young servant girls in the medieval images, give or take a few late exceptions. Nevertheless, they proliferated. Only a very few young girls or noblewomen appear in the written sources. They are seen welcoming visitors passing through and offering them baths, embroidering linens for the church, and sewing, while singing the "songs of the cloth" with their mother. We find them, more often in romances than in images, helping to weave ribbon by maintaining the threads of the woof. No doubt, they then helped to sew these beautiful strips onto the edges of civil or liturgical robes. "Go to your room to sew. That is the law of Nature . . ." the little Silence hears herself say at twelve years old, though she refuses to behave like a young lady. Unlike Silence, or even Christine de Pizan, who still complains as an adult of her mother only "wanting to occupy her with piles of thread," the daughters of nobility in general must have appreciated the various kinds of needlework, as much for their artistic value as for the ambiance of the women's quarters. For that matter, even if they were later destined to supervise a small band of servant girls, it was important for them to learn how to sew or to embroider. As Barberino remarks in his fourteenth-century *Régime des dames*, the daughters of knights, but also of judges and doctors, had every interest in mastering these skills, should they ever be subjected to a reversal in fortune.[18] In the best of conditions, he thinks, needlework would help make the idleness—completely relative, of course—of a noblewoman's life bearable.

Very small boys, who still lived with their mother and sisters, were probably not excluded from women's work. Women surely asked them to help, if only to keep them busy, as with the image of that model child, the Infant Jesus, who, in the illuminations, plays with bobbins of thread or balls of yarn and helps his mother making cloth. Adolescents also joined their mother in the women's quarters: the atmosphere there must have been warm and gay. In a twelfth-century text, written by Jean Renart, we see a young man, Guillaume, asking his mother to sing one of those "songs of the cloth," which women harmonized together while weaving and sewing: "Mother," interrupted Guillaume, "sing me a song, you will make me happy. . . ." Then she began in a pure, clear voice:

> Daughter and mother are embroidering,
> With gold thread, weaving golden crosses,
> The noble mother begins to speak
> Of how Aude burns with love for Doon!
>
> Daughter, learn how to sew and spin
> And to embroider gold crosses on the vestments.
> The love of Doon, you must forget.
> Of how Aude burns with love for Doon![19]

A good part of a woman's and her daughters' time was dedicated to the upbringing of little boys and taking care of the nursery, a good opportunity for young girls to practice before marriage. Unlike the children of common people who were closer to their fathers, these small boys were exclusively surrounded by female help: chamberwomen, nurses, cradle rockers, and even "women to relieve the night" for the newborn. They amused themselves, however, with war games. The little soldiers and knights made of metal or clay that we find in archaeological digs must have introduced them to the idea of war. They often left the women's quarters with their mother, their sister, or their nurse to watch their father returning from the hunt or from traveling, or to watch the physical exercises of big brothers and pages. In good weather, they played in the gardens, with water from the ornamental fountains, and, no doubt, pets. Dogs or cats, or even, among the highest nobility, monkeys and bear cubs, living stuffed animals, must have captured their attention. When they reached the age of reason, they were even forbidden from petting the kittens at mealtime, for hygienic reasons.

Thus, women and girls were not cloistered away in the women's quarters nor confined by their domestic tasks, anymore than little boys were. And contrary to the idyllic image the romances give of them, noble girls were hardly better behaved than those belonging to other social classes or other epochs. They indulged in pranks, sometimes cruel or even dangerous ones. In a book on upbringing dedicated to Marguerite de Bourgogne, a little eleven-year-old princess, Christine de Pizan mentions the bad manners of noble little girls who talk back to or even try to get rid of their governess by scattering dried peas on the stairs so she will "break her neck."[20] Nevertheless, it was their governess' job to entertain them, by telling them stories or fables and by playing with them, no doubt with pebbles and especially with dolls, such as archaeological digs have unearthed. The little girls were happy to have a squirrel, which a young peasant caught and tamed for them. This was a favorite animal of young noblewomen and girls. At court, little princesses, like Marie, the daughter of Charles le Téméraire, were fond of parrots. We know that girls also learned to ride horses, and then to hunt, notably with falcons, and especially that their intellectual training was sometimes as intensive as their brothers'. Indeed, at the castle, the reader was the woman. It was she who, from early childhood, prayed from her book of hours. It was the young girl of the house who took pleasure in reading novels, to herself, or out loud to the rest of her family. It was the woman who, later on, would learn to keep the records and check to see if the taxes had been paid correctly. The noblewoman was an intellectual, even a bibliophile, as were the queens and princesses of France, and in the most privileged circles, it was at a tender age, about five years old, that she was generally given her first book of hours or illustrated prayers. Painting and music were part of her education. If we are to believe the thirteenth-century authors, young, well-educated daughters of nobility learned how to perform, and also how to sing and to compose poems.

Good Manners

The behavior of young nobles, girls or boys, was regulated down to the smallest detail of daily life. According to Christine de Pizan, girls always had to hold themselves correctly, that is, always sitting or standing up straight, with a modest and reserved demeanor. They had to go to morning mass—which was not very difficult because castles commonly had a private chapel, complete with a chaplain—but on an empty stomach. They were even required to fast for many days each week when they were about to marry—but this was to quiet their adolescent ardor, and not to make them thin. They had to practice being polite toward everyone, the noble and the poor alike. Christine instructs the young Marguerite de Bourgogne not to be inconsiderate toward her servants: for her nighttime prayers, she must not get them up to make them light the candles, she must manage by herself. Appearance was carefully prescribed: clothes must not be too tight-fitting, out of concern for decency, hair must not fall across the cheeks; in fact, in the illuminations we see that the hair of noble daughters, left long, was braided or combed back into ponytails adorned with gold or silver jewels. However, there are plenty of examples of little girls or adolescents ignoring these various obligations and prohibitions. All the books of instruction meant for young girls give the same advice, which Christine herself must have read in her youth, in an old treatise from the fourteenth century, *The Book of the Knight of the Landry Tower for the teaching of his daughters.*[21]

Daughters were not the only ones to be given a proper upbringing: the behavior of boys was no less codified. But, smothered by the affections of mothers and big sisters, spoiled children were not uncommon. Educators and men of letters sometimes mention the tears and tantrums of little boys, indeed, even their brutality, which women try to recognize as early signs of a warrior's temperament. In fact, the violence of young knights is a character trait which is routinely noted.[22] In the very young, this behavior was no doubt even encouraged. In a "regimen" meant for nobility from the end of the thirteenth century, Aldebrandin of Sienna suggests that children must not be "put into a temper," "that what he asks for be granted him, and that nothing stand in his way or hold him back." In the fifteenth century, Olivier de la Marche evokes the early childhood of Charles, the future Téméraire, saying of him: "He was enthusiastic, lively, and frustrated as a child, and wanted to have every little thing done exactly his way." Fortunately, according to his chronicler, he "had so much sense and understanding that he resisted his temperament." Boys were taught to channel their emotions after the age of reason. Children were then subdued by the educators who, like Guibert de Nogent, taught them "modesty, propriety, and elegant manners," through the reading of books on comportment. Such manuals appeared throughout, in France, Italy, Spain, and England. They explained the proper ways to eat. In Spain, it was even forbidden to eat with "the whole mouth, but only with half, so as not to appear gluttonous"![23] Children were taught to hold themselves straight and to be quiet, but to smile when the lord entered the room where they happened to be. They learned how to answer his questions with responses full of deference, but also full of gaiety and good humor, a sentiment apparently considered characteristic of childhood (there were even women's recipes for "rendering a child beautiful and gay") and encouraged by preachers and mothers:

You are expected to be happy, you must be ready to respond with pretty words, sweet and respectful. . . . When you enter there where your lord is, say "God protect you," and, with modest acclamations, greet all those who are present. Do not burst in loudly, but enter with your head held high and a natural step, and kneel down only for your lord or sovereign, whichever he may be. . . . Answer your lord with reverence. Otherwise, hold yourself still as a rock, until he speaks. . . . If you see your lord drink, keep silent, without laughing aloud, whispering, whistling, joking, or any other kind of insolence. . . . When you are seated (at the table) do not tell crude stories. Avoid cleaning your nose, your teeth, or your fingernails at mealtime, as you have already been told. . . .[24]

"Apply yourself to constantly giving proof of your good upbringing," Tristan is advised by his teacher, a riding master who teaches him not only "the rules of courtesy," but also

among other things, how to play the harp and to sing. . . . He taught him to be generous with his fortune. . . . He taught him to speak as a man well brought-up and never to be lacking for words, and he told him that if he was foolish enough to be a liar, he would be scorned. He commanded him to be loyal as well. . . . He told him to be attentive in serving women with his arms and his fortune, with good humor.[25]

Finally, intellectual and artistic training were added to good manners.

Entertainment and Study: A Wise Mix

Children of nobility benefited from a diversified education. The records of the king René d'Anjou tell us how, in 1462–1464, at the castle of Bar, a "pastoral farce" was performed, and the actors in it were none other than his grandson, the future René de Lorraine, and the "children of the lords of the court."[26] Music, as well as drawing, were an integral part of their education and noble entertainment, and very young children trained in them, whether they were of nobility or not, like the image of little Benvenuto Cellini, who recalls in his autobiography how, at a "very tender" age, he was thus engaged to amuse the doge:

My father began to teach me the flute and vocal music. As I was still of a very tender age when children usually amused themselves with whistles or toys of this type, these paternal lessons caused me inexpressible displeasure, and it was only out of obedience that I resigned myself to playing the flute and to singing. . . . I was still very young at this time, and my father had me placed astride an usher's back to play the soprano flute with the palace musicians, before his Lordship. I read the pieces, perched on my porter. The ensign bearer took pleasure in making me babble, he gave me sugar-coated almonds.[27]

At the castle, boys as well as girls learned to dance, to sing, and to play the harp. Boys undoubtedly preferred practicing the chansons de geste, narrating glorious chivalric adventures, rather than the songs of the women's quarters, songs of the cloth or the cradle, which they nevertheless enjoyed listening to, as in the case of Guillaume, or composing, as in the case of the fifteenth-century prince poet, Charles d'Orléans. Nobles seem to have liked watching little children play and sing, a pleasure we can re-experience reading the furniture inventories of their castles, filled with tapestries "of the games of children," and silversmith's pieces "of children playing." Young nobility devoted themselves as well to more intellectual games: "tables" (that is, backgammon) and especially, chess. It was in playing this game, beginning from the age of seven, that they learned military strategy, but also its equivalent in civic training, courtesy—by playing with young girls and letting them win—and even mathematics. The game of chess seems a game of nobility *par excellence* because it employs royal courts, but also because it was apparently only played in castles and noble homes: not a single piece from this game has ever been discovered in farmhouse ruins. At the same time, this multifaceted diversion was useful for tempering the violence and passion of youthful nobility and for getting them interested in study and reflection.

The Classroom

In the castle, one room was devoted to the education of children. Did girls and boys study together under the iron rule of a single educator? Nothing is less certain. As in town, in the little schools, co-educational teaching seems to have been extremely rare. In the thirteenth century, Berthold de Ratisbonne distinguishes children by sex. Boys' masters he calls the "tutors of the high and mighty in this world, who are always close to them and teach them discipline and virtue.[28] And the little ladies have governesses who are with them all the time and teach them discipline and virtue very early." In the fifteenth-century court of king René d'Anjou, we also find that a man is paid "for having shown the hours to the little girls"—not to the girls and boys—that is, no doubt, for having given them a reading lesson from a book of hours, which included an alphabet and the important prayers. The educator, who was often the castle chaplain, had a difficult task in taking charge of a young boy whose entire environment prompted him to be restless. How could he sit still when his favorite horse was pawing in the stable? Rigorous methods were then called into play. No one seems to have been quite as brutal as the master of Guibert de Nogent, in the twelfth century, whom his mother had, nevertheless, gone to great trouble to hire away from a neighboring castle. Not only did he strike the child incessantly, but he even forbade him from playing with children his own age and kept him under "continual constraint, dressing him as a cleric."

> I watched the bands of playing children as if I were a being above them. I was hardly granted a few moment's rest, never a whole day, I was always overwhelmed with work as well, and my master was engaged to instruct only me.[29]

The "classroom" of the castle was furnished with a stool and bench for holding the books. Heated with a fireplace which provided both the warmth necessary for those who were forced to remain still and just enough light to read by, the room sometimes had a school board. A 1471 inventory of the castle of Angers mentions a "great board on which there are alphabets" in many languages. The master, standing, paced up and down the room, or even seated himself in a chair as a sign of his authority, while the student memorized the lessons. Great obedience was owed to the educator: the child called him *dominus*— my master, or my lord—and, like the little Lancelot in the illuminated manuscripts, often recited his lesson with one knee on the ground before him, learning the gestures of vassalage at the same time. Courts were no doubt given to fixed schedules, but there must have been many opportunities to escape, both for the educators as well as for the young students: indeed, Christine de Pizan recommends to the mother of high nobility that she take great care so "that the master is conscientious about making them learn for an adequate number of hours"[30]

An Individualized Learning Program

Beginning from Carolingian times, noble education had become a matter of the highest importance. An illiterate king is like a crowned ass, affirms Jean de Salisbury in the twelfth century. To show one's nobility, it was no longer sufficient to prove one's strength and courage or one's good manners. It was also necessary to be learned, to know—if possible—Latin, grammar, politics, history, even foreign languages. The educational program of nobles included all these disciplines: "Science and chivalry, which together suit many people very well," went the thirteenth-century saying. Noble youth were also given advice on lordly behavior, which they learned from tracts entitled "government of princes," or "mirrors of princes," of which the most famous models come from the program established by Vincent de Beauvais or by Giles of Rome for the children of Saint Louis and at his request.[31] These books were not suitable for the sons and daughters of simple bourgeoisie. At the end of the Middle Ages, the goal of educators was to make young nobles into "complete men," as athletic as learned, the ancestor of the modern day gentleman. But, no doubt, only a very affluent minority of the noble population was able to correspond to this ideal image of the educated knight. For that matter, even the sons of kings could not know everything, and Giles of Rome, who wrote a "prince's regimen" for Phillipe le Bel, explains:

> The sons of princes must know some theology, which is necessary to make them firm in their faith, and they must know especially the moral sciences which teach them to govern themselves and others. Of certain sciences, they must know that which can assist their moral development; of grammar, enough to understand the idiom in which moral and religious truths are taught; of rhetoric and the dialectic, that which will make their intelligence more quick, their manner of expression easier, of action, more powerful; of music, that which can bring them good morals. As

for the other sciences, it is enough for them to have a slight acquaintance with them.

These young privileged children were taught the model behavior of the heroes of romances. Like the young Tristan in the twelfth century, they were advised to avoid lying, which would cause them to be scorned, to be loyal, and "without ever failing in excellence, to always observe good manners and to act quickly and with discernment . . . to be attentive in serving women with his arms and his fortune, with good humor." Achievements, ability to make decisions, culture, a good education, and even a happy character: this was, therefore, the "profile" required of young nobles in the twelfth through fifteenth centuries.

TEN

The Child at School

Beginning from the twelfth century, nobles were no longer the only ones to be educated. It is often said that people of the Middle Ages were illiterate. But at that time, the term only referred to those who did not know Latin: medieval illiterates could know how to read, write, and do arithmetic! Thus, beginning from the second half of the twelfth century, even if only a few rural children regularly attended classes with the parish priest, a good number of city children already went to school. The practice of reading and writing was considered indispensable by many merchants and artisans. This medieval school is not the one of Guizot; in the fifteenth century, we must not, as yet, imagine long and regular schooling, but brief stays in very small establishments, for which one paid, or, more rarely, went free of charge—"the poor for God," reads a fifteenth-century notice. Even less must we imagine these schools to be secular. Even if, when the monastic school in Gand burned down in 1179, the laity rebuilt it and took charge of their children's education, even if anyone at all was allowed to open a little school, as in Ypres in 1253,[1] even if some masters in the fourteenth century were laymen, married and with families,[2] these cases were the exceptions to the rule.

Schooling

In the late Middle Ages, the Church still had the upper hand with regard to teaching. Most educators were clerics, sub-deacons, or parish priests. Primary and religious education were linked. Religious communities ran schools which were open to children of the bourgeoisie.[3] Moreover, though the bishops periodically stressed the need to send children to school, attending these establishments was not a legal obligation. However, there was no lack of encouragement: in 1179, the Third Latran Council ruled that in every cathedral, a master should be available to teach, without charge, not only the young clerics, but also students coming from the poorer classes; in 1215, the Fourth Latran Council ensured the training of masters, the clerics of parish churches. At the beginning of the fourteenth century, the bishop and liturgist, Guillaume Durand, of Mende, advocated that a school be opened in each village. In 1403, the synodical statutes ordered parish priests to require families to educate their children of six or seven years old, boys and girls, in the little urban schools, or even, in parishes which lacked schools, to entrust them to the parish priest who would teach them the bare essentials: the *Pater*, the *Ava Maria*, the *Credo*, and the *Benedicite*.[4] This type of injunction was repeated regularly, clear proof of the lack of primary schools, or of an incapacity on the part of parents, but also testimony to the constant concern of the men of the Church to educate the populace. But it is impossible to verify their effectiveness. Finally, until the thirteenth century at least, rural schools were only a limited phenomenon.[5]

We also do not know how many children went to school: no census is possible. However, based on fiscal and legal sources, medieval historians are now in agreement in thinking that, at the end of the Middle Ages, many more people knew how to read than was formerly believed. Indeed, there is no question that the number of schools and masters was grossly underestimated. In the case of the rural areas around Rheims, the registers only list those masters who had some business with the law! "There was no place in the historical records for schools with directors who led uneventful lives."[6] As for girls' schools, they are still more difficult to discern. Only by chance do schoolmistresses appear or not appear in archival sources, according to their family status. It is only when a woman is widowed that she is listed as the head of the family and that her profession is indicated. Otherwise, the silence of these sources is the rule. The education of girls is notoriously underestimated. Throughout the course of fiscal records schoolmasters appear. We know that in Lyon, besides the cathedral school, there were "little schools" in at least three collegiate churches as well as one hospital,[7] without counting a few parochial establishments about which we know nearly nothing. Such establishments only accepted a few students at one time; in a little school, such as those represented by illuminators beginning in the thirteenth century, six or seven children profit from the master's lessons. Rarely are classrooms portrayed as overcrowded, as in an illumination from the *Hours* of Louis de Savoie, from about 1460.[8] It contains about twenty little scholars crammed in, one against another. Some texts mention up to thirty-five names of students, as we see in a petition sent out by the students' parents in the town of Decize in 1336. Even if we knew the total number of schools, it would be impossible to calculate from that the numbers of pupils, because they were very variable, and even more impossible to deduce the total number of children taught to read and write, because there were other ways of learning to read outside of the schoolroom. Itinerant writers, who hired themselves out as private masters or tutors, and even lawyers, could supplement their income through this activity.[9] The situation with secondary schools is better known because the number of students was established in the statutes. Often these schools were maintained by public charity, and some of them only accepted poor students, or, failing that, those with some means who agreed to contribute to the general fund, as at Bons-Enfants, in Reims, in the thirteenth century.[10] The Collège de Hubant, established in Paris in the thirteenth century, accepted six students on scholarships between the ages of ten and twelve. The Collège de Bons-Enfants, in Reims, took twelve boarding students, ages nine to sixteen years. In Lyon in 1352, the cathedral ecclesiastical school took twelve students at a time as well.[11] And also, in Soissons in 1370, a school is opened on the rue de Bauton for twelve scholarship students.[12] This symbolic number is often exceeded. In the same city, the Collège de Soissons,

founded in 1345, is supposed to accept eighteen students,[13] and the same is true
for the Collège de Dix-Huit, in Paris, its name coming from its student enrollment.
Saint-Nicolas de Soissons accepted about sixty students, and Trets, in Provence,
counted no less than one hundred and eighty students, from the ages of twelve to
eighteen, in the fourteenth century. In these secondary schools, the students were
nearly exclusively male. The same was not always true for the "little schools." Few
texts, however, mention the school mistresses responsible for teaching little girls.
Co-education was not common practice. Only Froissart mentions it in his fourteenth-century verse autobiography, with regard to a school his parents forced
him to attend. But this situation is confirmed, in the negative, in the statutes of
scholarly establishments which required that school mistresses teach only girls.
This implies the possibility of co-education. It is true, though, that one hardly
forbids that which exists but proves to be in keeping with moral standards.

Literacy can sometimes be measured by the relatively high number of
schools, as in the Champagne region or in Paris. Thus, between 1460 and 1515 in
one Champagne diocese of three hundred parishes, there were thirty villages
which each had a school, and "schools were not the exclusive property of large
villages." Even a hamlet of only a dozen homesteads could have one. Thus, one
was able to speak of a "seedbed of rural schools," indeed, even, "a dense network
for rural education."[14] In Paris, in 1357, the first *Statuts* of the masters of the little
grammar schools demonstrate that the development of primary education there
was very important. They mention no less than about forty-one schoolmasters
and twenty-one schoolmistresses. At the rate of one master per school—because
classroom and school coincide, given the low number of students—that represents at least sixty-two establishments, since this list of masters may not be ex-
haustive.[15] We can better understand why it was forbidden for a school to be
opened in this city unless there were twenty houses between it and the next near-
est one in less populated neighborhoods, another indication of the importance
of academic institutions. The city of Reims seems to have offered a situation favorable for studies beginning from the thirteenth and fourteenth centuries. Little
schools were established there in even the smallest and poorest parishes, and
"many [of the bourgeoisie] knew how to read, write, and do arithmetic, at least in
the 14th century."[16] Reims benefited from the services of at least two school mistresses, listing one in the census of 1318, the other in 1328. In the fifteenth century
in Rouen, parish schools for children and grammar schools were established in
each neighborhood.[17] The most recent publication on thirteenth-century Germany confirms that "in all German towns, even the smallest ones, there were
public schools."[18] In northern Italy, schools for girls were opened as early as the
thirteenth century,[19] but this seems to be the exception. In Florence, "almost all
girls received no education other than that provided by their mothers, at home."[20]

The Level of Education

Thus, many children had access to the "basics," especially in towns, and, at
the end of the Middle Ages, even peasants learned to read. In certain rustic families, like this one from the Champagne region in 1474, "the four children of Jehan

inhabitants of Valenciennes in 1497 "might have been" literate, and in London in about 1500, it seems that "the majority of adults knew how to read and write,"[35] which means the literacy rate was considerably lower in the country. No doubt, this was also the situation in France. In the case of the Hesdin region, or of Aires sur la Lys, in the middle of the fourteenth century, there was, apparently, almost one school per parish, and, about 1500, 15 percent of the tenant farmers in a rural town in the Sambre valley were able to sign their names.[36] Let us note, however, that this does not mean that only 15 percent of the population could read and write. Married women had neither the opportunity nor the right to sign documents, and the same was true, of course, for children. But, just as the number of schools in the northern and eastern regions of France was especially high, in certain other areas, as in Tours, the situation appears to have been especially deplorable, at least immediately after the Hundred Years War. Thus, in 1432, and in 1439, schoolmasters were paid a salary, but the school, the only one, moreover, did not succeed in enrolling a hundred children, which would have allowed a schoolmaster and his aids to be assured a decent salary. It is true that education was not free, even if, in fact, one week's wages for a master builder could cover a child's schooling,[37] limited to a few months. It is not impossible that the English wars had temporarily disrupted elementary education, even if Philippe Contamine does not believe there was a general decline in education in this period. And it is not impossible, finally, that the situations were terribly out of balance between the northern and the southern regions of France, the north being better supplied with primary schools.

The Classrooms

What did the school look like? Texts and images allow us to enter the classroom. First of all, the premises: schoolmasters and mistresses held classes in ordinary houses, private residences. Perhaps a sign might indicate that this was a school house. In the fifteenth century, masters voluntarily hung advertising notices on their outside doors vaunting their qualifications, and the exceptional speed with which, they assured parents, they could teach children. Their signs, a few of which still survive, even though they were paper, willingly use seduction strategies. Competition was tough, in the fifteenth century, and the number of establishments rapidly increasing. Masters especially guaranteed gentleness in their teaching, which would tend to demonstrate that parents, who paid for their children's education, did not want to see their offspring thoughtlessly beaten. The text of these signs also appeals aggressively to even the poorest parents, promising them free schooling, as well as to the children: "Dear little ones of tender age, to learn to write well, apply great diligence, Devote your youth to it. . . ." Here is what one fifteenth-century schoolmaster from Toulouse says to them:

> There is a schoolmaster in this good city who . . . teaches how to read and write well, and to count and the numbers. . . . I will teach you well, truly and without trickery, you poor for God, you rich for money, you will

be received. For all this, come, all, very quickly, because I am bored with waiting so long and I am tired of saying this to you.[58]

These classrooms were of very various dimensions. In the fourteenth century in Lyon, we find a schoolmaster renting a "large house." But it is a simple "house" which "the lame woman who teaches the girls" keeps in the same town.[39] "House" is a very big word for what was, most of the time, only a room into which students were more or less comfortably crammed. This room, if we can believe the images, was sometimes below the street and vaulted. A small basement window supplied the only light, and it was probably not sufficient, all the more so because the school day began very early—five o'clock in the morning at Eton College, in England in the fifteenth century. Also, students were advised to have lamps: "a single lamp is sufficient for two children" we can read in the rules of one educational establishment. If this was the case throughout, it would provide us with some indication of the number of students. Thus, in 1471, in Séguret, the schoolmaster orders "three large lamps . . . and twenty-four small lamps" from a glassworker.[40] The classroom, small as it was, was quickly filled, even though it contained barely any school furniture. The only seating, even in the fifteenth century, was the cobbled floor, strewn with nothing but straw as protection against the dirt and cold, not a small thing in winter. Later, concerned with the children's discomfort, surely as detrimental to effective teaching as to health, we find that these stone basements were provided with flooring. Records, like for Lyon in 1545–1546, indicate that it was finally decided to "*poster*"—that is, to install a floor in—"the college classrooms which are paved with stone and make the little children very cold."[41] In fact, the only seat, which constituted the single piece of schoolroom furniture, was reserved for the master. This was "the chair." From this chair, he towered above his students who were seated on the floor, cross-legged, reading or writing on their knees. This chair was the symbol of his position, and no doubt, each school had one, because occasionally we find the schoolmaster protesting to the municipal authorities because his classroom is without one, and bluntly refusing to assume his teaching responsibilities if they do not provide him with this symbolic prop which must have helped him command respect. Finally, the master has at his disposal a complete range of instruments of coercion, which, the images show us, were not systematically employed. Often arranged against the chair's armrest, still more often held up as a sign of authority rather than aggression, we find a wooden ferule in the form of a large ladle or with a flat bowl, or a willow rod used as a preventative reminder to students that they must know their lessons by heart, without making any mistakes "in the rendering." The students thus sat on the floor in no very clear arrangement. The bigger ones helped the smaller ones, and the age levels were undoubtedly mixed. There was no rule, it seems, against the presence of domestic animals in the classroom—as, incidentally, was also true for the church—though they must have, nevertheless, distracted children from their studies. Little dogs, no doubt belonging to the schoolmaster, came to sit up and beg in front of this or that child, surely hoping for a crust of bread or some small treat.

Pupils had fewer accessories, because parchment, and even paper, were expensive. They were reserved instead for older scholars, who often wrote letters asking their parents for "some parchment, some ink, a writing case, and other objects which we need." In the little schools, on the other hand, lessons could be learned with empty hands. Many must have only had the master's book, a psalter or book of hours, with which each student took a turn practicing to read. In the Saint-Denis archaeological dig near Paris, a plaster alphabet disk has been found, which could surely have been inexpensively produced, and thus available to everyone. The student possessed a wax tablet, upon which he could write and erase as much as he wished, slates not showing up in student's leather schoolbags until the sixteenth century, if we can believe the written sources. Finally, on the classroom wall was sometimes hung a large board on which the master wrote the alphabet, or the music lesson. Most children did not have school books, and this board served as an economical substitute. If there were no board, a paper poster, like the one used for a sign, served the same purpose.

The School Day

If he was not a boarding student, the child left for school alone. The little scholar carried a sort of schoolbag, a "pocket" of colored material attached to his belt or furnished with a shoulder strap. His satchel filled with those accessories indispensable for writing exercises, the students left to go to the house of the schoolmaster or parish priest. Legal texts mention accidents which never failed to take place along the way. The schoolroom atmosphere did not correspond at all to the strict image we have construed of school in the distant past. For each good master, serious and well-educated, there were plenty of others who did not merit being entrusted with children. The itinerant schoolmaster was sometimes the reflection of those penniless, vagabond scholars who traveled all over Europe at that time. Some of them succeeded in tricking parents into hiring them, talking themselves into jobs, when they quite obviously possessed none of the qualities necessary for looking after children. Occasionally, parents bitterly complained about them, like the inhabitants of Decize, for example, in the Nevers diocese, who issued a petition to have the schoolmaster replaced. This schoolmaster, probably recruited in the usual way by ecclesiastical authorities, was, indeed, paid in part by the students' parents, who thus felt entitled to protest the way their children were being educated. We can understand why by reading their petition:

> We are certain that the aforementioned government [of Hugues of Bray, the schoolmaster] is neither good nor sufficient nor beneficial to the children of the aforementioned school, because the aforementioned students do not respect their master, and with all that, the aforementioned master, on the day of Saint Nicholas just past [the holiday of schoolchildren], gave and granted to these said students the right to play dice up to the sum of 12 *deniers* [and] they have become so used to this, that every day, they play dice at school openly and publicly before the aforementioned master . . . and when the master sometimes, out of shame, wants to correct them and

beat them for this, they defend themselves and strike him with stones or other things or jab him with their pens, these children of fourteen year or thereabouts.[42]

Obviously, all medieval schools were not transformed into gambling casinos. Written records inform us that in the most serious cases, all the more serious because of this, the offending schoolmasters were usually clerics. On the other hand, the regulations of some educational institutions specified the qualities required of schoolmasters and mistresses. Morality and competence were written into the statutes, as, for example, in Paris. Schoolmasters did not have the right to teach grammar if they were not good enough grammarians—which also means they had to be Latinists. They had to teach the children their letters "painstakingly." They were forbidden from attracting students away from or speaking ill of a colleague. They were not allowed to live with a woman of ill-repute (!) and must not overcrowd their classrooms: "if someone goes over the fixed number of students" the excess revenue was simply confiscated.[43]

In the secondary schools, students boarded, partly because they were poor or sometimes came from far away. They had no other choice, unlike the children in the lower schools who returned home at the end of the day. For these children, too, boarding was possible. The notice of a fourteenth-century schoolmaster proclaims that

> The writer accepts children as boarders
> Showing them how to write properly
> To trim their quill pens and to read well
> And all manner of good education.[44]

Everyday life for the scholar no doubt followed the usual schedule of the medieval world: rising early, retiring early, two daily meals punctuating the day. Boarding students slept in beds filled with straw, set up in dormitories without light or heat, but with blankets. At Bauton de Soissons, the dormitories each held six beds.[45] At the College de l'Ave-Maria, in Paris, students slept two to a bed. An amusing text from a bit later, tells how the school day of a boarding student begins; this is from 1565, by a student named Mathurin Cordier:

> After I woke, I got out of bed, I put on my doublet and *saye* [tunic]. I sat down on a stool, I took my knee breeches and my long pants, as I had both kinds, I took my shoes, I attached my breeches to my doublet with the aglets, I attached my low pants with garters above the knees, I took my belt. I combed my hair, I took my hat and arranged it well, I put on my robe, and then, having left the chamber, I went downstairs, I peed [*sic*!] in the courtyard against a wall, I took water from a bucket, I washed my hands and my face with a towel.

Another unusual document, involving the College de Trets in 1364–1365,[46] which was founded by Urbain V, evokes with rare detail the daily diet of the young scholar, and even describes the olfactory ambiance of his place of study, scented with the good smell of warm bread, baked in the college oven, and the aroma of cabbage, served in soup 302 days out of 365. The daily menus included a bit of wine, a little more than a half-liter, which was very little for this period, and is explained by the young age of those it was allotted to—and a little more than a pound of bread per student. Students were allowed one soup daily—two during Lent—of cabbage, spinach, beans, leeks, or squash, seasoned with a bit of cheese, grated, no doubt. They were fed ample amounts of fresh meat, essentially mutton, and fish or eggs during Lent. A few fruits, figs, walnuts, plums completed the fairly balanced, but not very varied meals, except during the major holidays: Easter lamb and Christmas omelets brightened the everyday fare, no doubt intentionally stripped of all extras. Such precise records allow us to do an actual dietary analysis of the student menu: about 2,600 daily calories, which is fully adequate for a sedentary young adolescent, a supply of mineral elements rich in iron, but low in glucides, vitamins B, C, and D. At Trets, the cook was careful to balance the meals, alternating fresh and dried vegetables regularly, preferring fresh meat to salted meat, cooked only one day out of six. To respond to the legendary appetite of young boys, he compensated for the absence of meat during Lent by providing twice as much vegetable soup. However, dairy products, considered essential for adolescents today, were curiously absent. Some other bits of information complete this dietary panorama. At Bauton, a school in Soissons, the students ate peas, eggs, and feasted on a pig at Christmas. Their bread was made of "better wheat" and the purchase of condiments permitted them to season the soups.

The illustrated regulations of little scholars from the College de l'Ave-Maria, in Paris, give some additional information on the life of boarding students, ages ten to twelve. At the great festivals, one of the students holds a candle and finds himself rewarded with a *pinte* of wine, a loaf of bread, a bowl of soup, and half a side of meat. The children had to participate in acts of mercy, death watches, prison visits, helping to give clothes, shoes, and food to the poor. They accompanied burials. At school, they had to sweep up in front of the altar of the Virgin, refill the oil lamps in the chapel, and clean the bird cages. They said their prayers already lying down under the covers, because of the cold, and one of the children had the nightly responsibility of ringing the bell from his bed for saying the *Ave Maria* in honor of the patron saint of the institution.

It does not seem as though life in boarding school was at all easy for children. Out of sight, out of mind; parents seem to have had some tendency to forget about them there. The boarders often had to make appeals to their families begging for clothes or accessories needed to pursue their studies, and we still have a few of these letters from students:

> To his very dear father David, Matthieu, your son in body and spirit, greetings and filial blessings. Do not be astonished, do not be irritated, if you receive frequent letters from me expressing my complaints. . . . Your benevolence knows well that when you sent me to school, you let me

leave with only four sous to give to the master, you did not give me what was necessary and sufficient by way of clothing, and you have since sent me nothing more.

Students did not limit themselves to asking for a change of clothes, "shoes and breeches," or to begging their fathers to be good enough to pay the master. They also kept their parents informed of their progress and their health. Suspicious, some parents, like the fifteenth-century English family, the Pastons, sometimes had their children watched, learned that they devoted themselves too avidly to the pleasures of chess, and wrote, in their turn, to complain.

We do not know if the school day usually included periods of free time, in addition to mealtimes. It is likely that, when an important personage, a lady of nobility, for example, came to visit the school, she ordinarily granted the students a recess. On the students' holiday, the feast of Saint Nicholas, children were allowed to play—and bad masters, like the one in Decize, allowed them to play the forbidden game of dice. At the end of the day, or during "vacations," the teacher surely used his free time to straighten the school or restock school supplies, like this English schoolmaster who "stole away after the meal to find rods to beat his students with." Immanent justice: he fell from the willow tree he had been climbing and drowned in a mill pond.

Punishments and Amusements

To what kind of masters, then, were children entrusted? The written sources sometimes leave us perplexed as to how humane they were, in their everyday behavior as well as in their educational training, often very slight. It is true that legal sources are our primary source of information about the actions and incidents involving these schoolmasters, and that they are generally mentioned for their atrocious conduct. Since good masters are not spoken of there, we see only the bad side: excessively severe masters striking children or excessively lenient masters setting bad examples for them. That is the case with the village schoolmaster in Charny who is arrested for having played dice, which was illegal, and considered indecent even though it was a very popular pastime.[47] Despite the pervading laxness, corporal punishment was not uncommon; there can be no doubt about that. Too many examples remain, in legal records as well as in images, of young dunces being punished, for us to imagine school life being as sheltered as it is today. However, it seems that only the bad students were struck, never the very youngest among them, and that excessive beatings were forbidden. It was even recommended to strike "gently": beating a student was permitted, but not injuring him. All the same, certain thirteenth- and fourteenth-century schoolmasters, still under the influence of the old traditions of monastic severity, continued to beat children, like Etienne de Aubazine in the twelfth century, "with a blow of a stick on the head, or of a hand across the face in such a way that the noise of it rang in every ear, especially if it was a matter of a little child, in order to correct him and to terrify the others."[48] However, as we see in the writings of Saint

Anselm, consulted on this point by an instructor of young monks, all masters did not consider it good to strike students, which only served, to use his words, to make them "completely dazed." They first applied themselves to channeling the children's energy. Before beginning to work, the good master "settles [the children] down," says Froissart in *L'Espinette amoureuse*, a text in which he recounts his memories of childhood. To cajole students and interest them in schoolwork, some fourteenth-century schoolmasters favored a playful approach to teaching. Master Yon, an instructor at Soissons, made use of mnemonic devices, jokes, and word games to put his students at ease. Already in the twelfth century, Master Egbert of Liège taught children grammar with the help of amusing little stories, among which we find the precursor to "Little Red Riding Hood."[49] Thus, laughter and smiles were not entirely absent from these institutions which did not all constitute "jails for captive youth," as Montaigne calls them in the sixteenth century, driven by a whipping master with the evocative name of Tempeste. Texts show us that children indulged in jokes of questionable taste, often at the expense of the master, playing at cutting his mustache during his nap, or pulling out his tongue. With age, this behavior does not seem to come to an end, and we even find a twelfth-century priest of Bourg-Saint-Remi striking and excommunicating some novices from Rheims who were making fun of him.[50] This sentence, needless to say, was revoked.

Learning the alphabet itself led to amusing, indeed even scatological digressions, which must have made unruly children laugh. A little fifteenth-century poem, *La Ballade de l'ABC*,[51] shows us how the pronunciation of letters led to jokes, notably for the Q, [pronounced "*cul*" which is the word for backside] because, "*par Q, vente, tonne et espart.*" This letter was considered a "bad letter" and if it was supposed to be "naughty to name the Q," no doubt children delighted in doing so. A little medieval riddle asks "is the abc [pronounced "*abbesse*," meaning abbess] male or female throughout?" The answer is unambiguous: "I tell you indeed it must be female, because we find there *cul et quon et point de vit* [backside and "*quon*" and no penis].[52] This mysterious "*quon*" probably goes back to *cum* (with), for which the French pronunciation evokes the female sexual organs. Actually, little students were also learning by heart the principal abbreviations used in writing, always included at the end of the alphabet. Other jokes, more innocuous, make the O the open-mouthed letter of astonishment: "O marvels late or soon" and do the same for A: "When my master said AAA, I thought that he was *ébahi* [dumbfounded]" says the ballad. Indeed, reciting the alphabet began by enunciating the letter A three times. The poet, who is apparently remembering his childhood, makes the L [*aile*—wing] a sought-after delicacy: "L of plump capon is good." The unruly student is warned against the letter D [*dés*—dice]: "D is a bad letter and has done many a cleric harm," who have lost their habits to this game. We have seen that bad masters did not deny themselves, all the same. The ballad of the alphabet ends with a formula which undoubtedly appeals to its potential audience, the sons of merchants: "*Car en trestout mon abc/ n'a bonne lectre sinon G* [j'ai—I have, or I possess]. As with this amusing alphabet, it is in French that children in the lower schools of the late Middle Ages learned to express themselves, because they were not taught Latin. To become a merchant or artisan, then, it was not at all necessary to learn grammar, a study reserved for the upper schools and for children destined, instead, for the clergy.

To diversions were added vacations, which broke up the time in school. They were called *"vaccations."* In Soissons, school began again after the grape harvest, in October, no doubt to allow students from the country to return to help their families—we have almost retained this agrarian calendar. Like all other activities, schooling yielded to the demands of the Christian calendar. Christmas vacation lasted fifteen days, and Easter vacation, ten days. At Soissons, student scholarships were granted for forty-four weeks, thus corresponding to the length of a school year. No doubt, school was also suspended for public holidays, which represented nearly a third of the year. As for those who did not like school, they deliberately played hooky, and it was necessary, according to school regulations, to have monitors to make sure that students did not take off for the rivers, in good weather, to indulge in the pleasures of bathing. In an autobiographical work written about 1450, the English poet, Lydgate, remembers that he liked to get to school late, out of pure ill-will, and that rather than study, he abandoned himself to the pleasures of jokes or childhood quarrels which exasperated the masters, or even going to steal apples from the gardens or strip grapes from the vines.[53]

The Children's Opinion

So it happens that the principal players have left only a few autobiographical indications of the pleasure—or more often, the displeasure—they felt with regard to school. The rare pleasure, for Froissart, of delighting the little girls at a school, for once, agreeably co-educational, by offering them "a lock of hair, or even an apple or a pear, or even just a little glass ring,"[54] more often displeasure at finding himself obliged to study instead of going to play in the streets or the fields. The avowed pleasure of skipping school for Lydgate, who, in an autobiographical text, recalls his childhood motto: "Whereof rebuked, this was my device."[55] In a thirteenth-century text, the author of the German version of the *Romance of Tristan*, Gottfried, flatly pronounces the educational process of his time to be "a yoke imposed beginning from the age of seven years, which robs them of their freedom, weighs them down with cares, and makes all their joy wither."[56] These are the same terms the Italian merchant, Giovanni Morelli, uses, when he evokes his childhood. To him, education was "hard on the freedom of childhood." Gottfried does not hesitate to say that "the better part of their life" is taken away from children. Reading some thirteenth-century secondary school statutes makes it easier to understand the reasons behind these bad memories. The order is strict, almost monastic. The little scholar was often tonsured. The students at Bons-Enfants of Reims were required to wear gray cloaks and to go begging in town for the daily bread for the school, to remain silent during meals, to speak among themselves only in Latin, and to submit to discipline each night.[57] Not all of them had suitable living conditions. Students in Toulouse were lodged in hospitals and were not provided with sufficient bedding. In Agen, some students were housed in an old prison.[58]

Nonetheless, all children were not subjected to such a regime. At the end of the thirteenth century, Aldebrandin of Sienna advises noble French mothers that it is necessary to send a child to school at the age of seven "and to entrust him to a master who knows how to teach him without beating him and with whom he doesn't have to be too strongly forced to stay against his will."[59] This was, no doubt, a devout wish, applying more to the lower schools than to the colleges marked with austerity.

* * *

Children in the country, children in town, children of medieval castles, or rural youth sent to town to do apprenticeships or go to school. . . If the first of these remained on the farm with their parents until they were fairly old, often until the age of marriage, which, for boys, did not take place until they were about thirty, the other categories of youth, *a priori* very different, had one characteristic in common. All of them had the opportunity or the obligation to leave their families when they were still children. Thus, little nobles left to go learn their future "trade" of knighthood at another residence. At adolescence, those who had the means left the family castle to travel, as a way of completing their education.[60] Like Tristan in the twelfth century, they wanted to go visit foreign countries. This young hero's teacher advises him, "Ask your father to grant you permission to go see foreign countries. It would not be good if you go without knowledge of foreign countries," and the young man asks his father straight out for authorization to go away:

> Dear father, consent to let me leave. To wait longer does me wrong. . . . I would like to leave to present myself to the greatest possible number of unknown people, be it for serious business, be it for diversion. I would not be upset if I happened upon some difficult trial. At my young age, I must go to see how one lives in foreign countries.

Many young nobles actually did make such voyages, but so did the sons of merchants, motivated by other reasons. Young artisans also left their families. They were placed in apprenticeships, sometimes far from home. Orphans had no other choice but to go learn a trade from an outsider. The sons and daughters of peasants sometimes also left for apprenticeships, but they were not placed very far from their homes, as in the case of a little Jeannette, eleven years old, who goes to work as a chambermaid three leagues from the house where she was born. Future scribes or artists travel long distances, like the Ancône apprentice who writes jokes in German in the margins of the book he is given to copy. Children go along on pilgrimages, especially at the end of the Middle Ages, indeed even going alone, as was the case with the "children's crusade" which attracted a few older adolescents—adults according to medieval standards—but primarily children. Or again, with the spontaneous pilgrimage of the children of Mont-Saint-

Michel, which, at the end of the fourteenth century, cast out onto the road children "all or for the most part virgins . . . without having taken leave of either father or mother, without money, without bread or wine." There is, in these wanderings, more often than not planned, a distinctive characteristic of the medieval world, the desire for an introduction to independence and autonomy. The adolescent runaway, no doubt relatively common in the Middle Ages, was another manifestation of this independence. This was not necessarily an escape from family or a disastrous professional situation. It was also a way of putting oneself to the test. Mathaeus Schwarz, a young man of good family, recalls in his illustrated autobiography how he ran away at nine years old, about 1505, and made his way singing under the windows of noble ladies. In reality, to change families, to travel, to run away, are so many ways of discovering once again how to do things, of opening horizons. Travels shape the young, the expression still goes. This is the distant echo of a typical situation in the Middle Ages.

Actually then, the only kind of mobility which could be said to be forbidden to the young was social mobility. In a chanson de geste written at the end of the twelfth century, we can read the following advice: "Do not make a bishop out of the son of your shepherd. Choose the son of a king, a duke, a count, or even the son of a vavasor. . . . Leave the villain to his furrow, because the villain has only to be given a stronghold, and his nature always ends up taking over again." That is an opinion which is going to persist. "A child must be taught such a trade as suits his social position" says Philippe de Novare at the end of the thirteenth century. Even though the same author also insists upon the fact that, "it can happen that the son of a poor man becomes a cleric, which is often the case, and can thus become a great prelate; and thus become rich and honored, and father and sire to him and his own, and command all those in that country and can become pope, and be father and sire to all Christianity," in reality, the son of a peasant only rarely becomes a pontiff or a theologian like Jean Gerson. And the counter-example of Gerbert, the son of Cantal peasants who was taken into the Aurillac monastery very young and became pope in the year 1000, cannot be considered the general rule, especially in the last three centuries of the Middle Ages. Changing one's position was not impossible, however. Entrusted to a monastery by his parents, the little peasant was authorized to become a monk, and this way of rising in society, which, moreover, kept him safe from dangers and food shortages, must have been a strong impetus for many parents to offer their sons as oblates. Apart from this exception, the young had hardly any opportunities for gaining social status. Only the peasants in a few regions of the midwest of France could accede to nobility. In the time of Saint Louis, in Forez and in Vivarais, there were well-to-do *"paysans fieffés,"* from among whom knights were sometimes recruited. And in Italy, certain rural folk could still aspire to one day owning a great house, land, and a name, and, over a few generations, hope to rise from their rural state to minor nobility. In contrast, a few nobles worked with their hands. They were metallurgists or glassworkers, a trade theoretically reserved for nobility.[61] In Languedoc, it was by royal order that this activity was reserved for "gentlemen," "noble and from noble stock," and, moreover, only on the condition that they themselves were the sons of glassworkers. Even the bastard sons of nobility were denied the right to practice this profession which could, however, be passed down through the mother serving as intermediary, and which was opened to legitimate daughters.

But these are the exceptions which prove the rule, a rule which thirteenth-century texts never tired of repeating, featuring rural youths who, rejecting their state in life, leave to find their fortune and play the knight. But, surely to please noble readers, the story always ends badly, and the peasant son, ashamed and confused, finally accepts his rustic condition. In Germany, this is the argument of the romance of *Helmbrecht the Farmer*, in France, at the beginning of the thirteenth century, of *Courtois d'Arras*. Courtois, the son of a stockbreeder, sadly misnamed for a simple peasant, refuses to accept his situation, demands his part of the inheritance, leaves for the city, ruins himself drinking and gambling, and ends up . . . as a swineherd, that is, worse off than he was before. He finally returns, repentant, to his father's house.[62] The moral is that one must not try to change one's state. Or at least not all at once. This does not stop the son of a farmer from being allowed to enter secondary school, especially if, like little Peter, he was considered "too weak of arm to be able to learn a trade,"[63] a chance for the puny child to climb the social ladder. In artisan circles, placement in an apprenticeship with a professional whose trade was related to, but considered more prestigious than their father's also allowed youths to elevate themselves slightly. The son of the blacksmith became a silversmith; the son of a silversmith did not always adopt his trade. He could become a great painter, like Domenico Ghirlandaio, in the fifteenth century. Among the various branches of the arts and crafts, ways were open, at least to the young person in the process of being trained. To be convinced of this, we need only to observe the fate of the famous Limbourg brothers, the favorite painters of Jean de Berry, who were placed in an apprenticeship as "young children" with a Parisian silversmith,[64] but changed course as adolescents to become illuminators for the court.

In the fifteenth century, more and more, the shopkeepers dreamed of nobility for their sons, who became rich merchants and bought letters of ennoblement, indeed even feudal estates. Business wealth also permitted this rise in social status, for so long denied to the children of commoners, at least to a certain extent. For Jacques Le Goff, "social mobility in the medieval business world was not as great as it has sometimes been said to be," even for the sons of merchant bankers.[65] But if nobility and the rich bourgeoisie tended to merge, the peasants were excluded from this phenomenon more than ever, indeed even scorned. At the end of the Middle Ages, only the cultivation of the mind in conjunction with that of the fields still permitted rural youth some hope of rising above their circumstances, for example, by becoming priests. Indeed, it was primarily education, which more and more "ignoble" children received, that granted them a (very) relative degree of parity with young nobles. *Scolae, scalae*, it was said: school was a ladder which let children surmount their birth. Those in power were aware of this. In the fourteenth century, a few found or orphaned children were taken in by the Court, and endowed by dauphins and princes who put them "into schools to learn"—but what became of these children as adults? Whatever the case may be, birth was in the process of losing its importance. It was no longer sufficient reason to be owed respect. The adages, which warned children of high nobility that no one could be admired for their birth alone if they were not also literate, proliferated. We can even read that "the son of a chambermaid, well taken to task, is worth quite a bit more than the son of a king who is badly brought up," according to the pen of the author of *Jehan de Saintré*, an initiation romance written by Antoine de la Sale in 1456, and meant for young people, the hero of which is a young boy of thirteen who makes an apprenticeship of courtesy.[66]

This was a new vision, nearly unthinkable before then. An Italian grammarian, Milo da Colla, considers that, in his opinion, learning pulled the poor out of the dust, that it ennobled the non-noble and conferred upon them an illustrious reputation. Humanism brought about a—very relative—disruption in the *ordo*. And, in fact, education, if it did not transform the ignoble into nobility, did put everyone on equal footing. The cultivated merchant understood this well, and no long felt belittled before the noble. Thus, as the fifteenth century progressed, the idea that the merchant possessed some degree of dignity increasingly took hold.[67] This new dignity came, essentially, with schooling, or with talent, and one Benvenuto Cellini, born "in humble conditions," as he himself said, was well and truly accepted into Florentine nobility fifty-four years later.

CONCLUSION

Having reached the end of this work, the reader may have the impression that it is very difficult to map out a history of childhood in the Middle Ages. Up until the thirteenth century, the sources deriving principally from clerics are short on information about everyday life, and our perception of medieval childhood is significantly altered according to the type of document considered, the social class under observation, the geographical area under study, the age or sex of the child, and the time period in question. Also, rather than a history of childhood, we must speak of *childhoods*, because this is certainly a matter of a history with many levels. However, a few basic features emerge from this study, and it is useful to conclude by summarizing them briefly here.

First of all, let us abandon for good the idea of a lack of feeling for children in the Middle Ages. Despite often difficult living conditions, the great majority of children, within their families, at school, in monasteries, with a patron or a lord, in the street or in the fields, were surrounded with affection and carefully educated. Furthermore, the child and the family in the Middle Ages represented a whole set of specific things which stemmed primarily from the importance of Christian religion within the society. Finally, medieval childhood was characterized by some particular living conditions, which did not always involve the family. The child had many opportunities to leave his natural family in order to be looked after by adults other than his father and mother, who, nevertheless, accepted their roles. In addition, it must be admitted that to study children only within the family unit formed by these two parents is not at all sufficient. The historian must look at the "supporting" structures of the society as well, such as the blended family, the business, or the monastery. All these adoptive families succeeded one another in loving, rearing, and educating children. They played a fundamental role in the apprenticeship of life, and this phenomenon as a whole demonstrates that all of medieval society was involved in the life of the child.

NOTES

Introduction

1. Ph. Ariès, *L'Enfant et la vie familiale sous l'Ancien Régime* (Paris: Plon, 1960; new ed. 1973).

2. Ibid, p. 29.

3. Ibid., introduction, p. xi.

4. P. Riché, *Education et culture dans l'Occident barbare (VIe–VIIIe siècles)* (Paris: Seuil, 1962).

5. J.-L. Flandrin, "Enfant et société," *Annales ESC* 19, no. 2 (March–April 1964): 322–329.

6. E. Le Roy Ladurie, *Montaillou, village occitan de 1294 à 1324* (Paris: Gallimard, 1975), ch. 13, pp. 300–323.

7. "L'enfant à travers les siècles," interview with Ariès, remarks recorded by M. Winock, *L'Histoire* 19 (January 1980): 86.

8. E. Shorter, *Naissance de la famille moderne, XVIIIe–XXe siècles* (Paris: Seuil, 1977; original version, 1975), pp. 210–218.

9. E. Badinter, *L'Amour en plus. Histoire de l'amour maternel, XVIIIe–XXe siècle* (Paris: Flammarion, 1980), pp. 34 and 67.

10. For critiques of the thesis of Ariès, refer in particular to D. Alexandre-Bidon, "Grandeur et renaissance du sentiment de l'enfance au Moyen Age," *Educations médiévales, l'enfance, l'école, l'Eglise en Occident (VIe–XVe siècles)*, special issue of the review *Histoire de l'Education*, INRP (1991): 39–63.

11. See the works cited in the bibliography.

12. For a study of childhood beginning from iconography, see D. Alexandre-Bidon and M. Closson, *L'Enfant à l'ombre des cathédrales* (Lyon: PUL-CNRS, 1985).

Part I
ONE *The Christian Family and Relations*

1. See, in particular, N. Belmont, "Levana ou comment "élever" les enfants" *Annales ESC*, no. 1 (January–February 1973): 77–89.

2. Saint Augustine, *De sancta virginitate*, book I, ch. III, *Patrologie Latine (PL)*, 40, col. 398.

3. Saint Augustine, *Confessions*, ed. P. Labriolle (Paris, 1947, reissued 1966), I, IX, t. I, p. 16.

4. Jacques de Voragine, *La Légende dorée* (Paris: GF-Flammarion, 1967), t. I, p. 47.

5. *Gesta abbatum Orti sancte Marie*, ed. A. W. Wybrands (Leeuwarden, 1879), p. 5.

6. P. Veyne, "La famille et l'amour sous le Haut Empire roman," *Annales ESC* (1978): 35–63.

7. Grégoire de Tours, *Histoire des Francs*, ed. R. Latouche (Paris: Les Belles Lettres, 1963), t. I, V. 21.

8. Bède la Vénérable, *Histoire ecclésiastique du peuple anglais*, ed. and trans. P. Delaveau (Paris: Gallimard, 1995), p. 110.

9. Ibid., p. 147.

10. J. Gélis, *L'arbre et le fruit, la naissance dans l'Occident moderne, XVIᵉ–XIXᵉ siècle* (Paris: Fayard, 1984), p. 57.

11. J.-Cl. Schmitt, *Le saint Lévrier. Guinefort, guérisseur d'enfants depuis le XIIIᵉ siècle* (Paris: Flammarion, 1979), p. 112.

12. Cited in J. Berlioz, "Pouvoir et contrôle de la croyance: la question de la procréation démonique chez Guillaume d'Auvergne," *Razo 9* (Nice) (1989): 16.

13. Burchard de Worms, *Decretum*, book XIX, *Corretor sive medicus*, PL 140, col. 537–1058, canon 179. Translation in C. Vogel, *Le pécheur et la pénitence au Moyen Age* (Paris: Cerf, 1969), pp. 87–93.

14. Grégoire de Tours, *Liber II de virtutibus S. Martini*, published in *Monumenta Germaniae Historica (MGH)*, *Scriptores Rerum Merovingicarum (SRM)*, I, p. 617.

15. Paul Diacre, *Histoire de Lombards* (Paris: Les Belles Lettres, 1995), book I, 15, p. 20.

16. *Le Frêne. Lais de Marie de France*, trans. L. Harf-Lancner, ed. Karl Warnke, Lettres gothiques (Paris: Le Livre de Poche, 1990), pp. 89–91. Twins are not always regarded in a negative way. Some literary texts also portray them as particularly valued beings.

17. Bède, *Histoire ecclésiastique du peuple anglais*, p. 107.

18. *La vie et les miracles de saint Amator*, ed. E. Albe (1909), book II, 29.

19. Bède, *Histoire ecclésiastique du peuple anglais*, pp. 106–107.

20. *Corpus christianorum*, ed. G. Morin, t. CIII (1953), pp. 9, 196, 229, and 231.

21. Burchard de Worms, *Decretum*, article 159; C. Vogel, *Le pécheur et la pénitence*, p. 106.

22. Hermannus, *Liber de restauratione Sancti Martini Tornacensis*, c. 18, *MGH, Scriptores in-fol. (SS)*, t. XIV, p. 282.

23. J.-L. Flandrin, *Un temps pour embrasser, aux origines de la morale sexuelle occidentale (VIᵉ–XIᵉ siècle)* (Paris: Seuil, 1983), pp. 48–49.

24. *Pénitentiel du Pseudo Bède*, II, 4, PL 94, col. 571.

25. Mansi, *Sacrorum conciliorum nova et amplissima collectio, in fol.* (Florence and Venice, 1759–1798), t. IX, p. 997.

26. *Vita Leobae abbatissae biscofesheimensis, auctore Rudolfo, MGH, SS*, t. XV, p. 127.

27. The same causes are found at the end of the Middle Ages. See J.-B. Brissaud, "L'infanticide à la fin du Moyen Age: ses motivations psychologiques et sa répression," *Revue historique du droit français et étranger* 50, no. 2 (April-June 1972): 229–256.

28. J. Boswell, *Au bon coeur des inconnus. Les enfants abandonnés de l'Antiquité à la Renaissance* (Paris: Gallimard, 1993) (English ed., 1988).

29. Réginon de Prum, *Libri duo de synodalibis causes et disciplinis ecclesiasticis*, ed. F. Wasserschleben (Leipzig, 1840), p. 68.

30. Boswell, *Au bon coeur des inconnus*, pp. 117–120.

31. Grégoire de Tours, *Histoire des Francs*, t. I, V, 17.

32. Ibid., t. II, IX, 20.

33. *Leges Visigothorum*, ed. K. Zeumer (Hanover, 1902), 4.4.3.

34. Canon 60 of the Council of Toledo IV in 633, published by J. Vives, *Concilios visigoticos e hispano-romanos* (Barcelona and Madrid, 1963), p. 212.

35. Ch. Fell, *Women in Anglo-Saxon England* (Oxford: Basil Blackwell, 1987), p. 82.

TWO **The Christian Child**

1. *S. Hieronymi Presbyteri Opera, Pars I, Opera exegetica 7, Commentarium in Matheum, Libri IV, III* (Typographi Brepols, 1969), p. 157. This commentary is also found in Colomban, Bede, or Isidore of Seville: see Riché, *Education et culture*, p. 505, note 50.

2. *Sermon VII*, 3–4.

3. Isidore of Seville, *Etymologiae*, XI, 2–10, ed. W. M. Lindsay (Oxford, 1911).

4. I. H. Fosyth, "Children in Early Medieval Art: Ninth through Twelfth Centuries," *Journal of Psychohistory* 4, no. 1 (summer 1976): 32.

5. Bède, *Histoire ecclésiastique du peuple anglais*, p. 168.

6. Amalaire, *Liber Officialis*, v. 29, 11, ed. Hanssens, *Amalarii episcopi opera liturgica omnia*, t. I, *Studi et testi* 138 (Rome, 1948), p. 499.

7. Grégoire de Tours, *Histoire des Francs*, t. II, VIII, 16.

8. *De vita et miraculis sancti Goaris*, 20, *PL* 121, col. 649.

9. Benedict de Peterborough, *Miracles de Thomas Becket*, ed. J. G. Robertson, *Materials for History of Archbishop Thomas Becket*, Rolls Series no. 67, vols. 1 and 2, (1875), book II, 25.

10. *Vita Sancti Aniani III*, ch. 2, in *Saint Aignan et le siège d'Orléans par Attila*, ed. A. Theiner (Paris, 1832), p. 34.

11. Jean de Salisbury, *Polycraticus*, II, cap. XXVIII, *PL* 199, col. 474.

12. *Vita Benedicti, Acta Sanctorum (AS)*, April II, 225.

13. Julien de Vézelay, *Sermons*, ed. D. Vorreux, "Sources chrétiennes" (1972), t. I, no. 192, p. 309.

14. Guibert de Nogent, *Autobiographie*, ed. E. R. Labande (Paris: Les Belles Lettres, 1981), I, VI, p. 122.

15. On the ambiguity noted here, see D. Lett, "Le corps de la jeune fille. Regards de clercs sur l'adolescente aux XIIe et XIVe siècles," *Le temps des jeunes filles, Clio*, no. 4 (autumn 1996): 51–73.

16. Gervais de Tilbury, *Le Livre des Merveilles*, ed. and trans. A. Duchesne (Paris: Les Belles Lettres), no. 103, pp. 112–128.

17. Saint Augustine, *Les Confessions*, I, 7, 11, t. I, p. 9.

18. Abélard, *Historia Calamitatum*, ed. J. Monfrin (Paris: J. Vrin: new ed., 1978), p. 76.

19. Saint Augustine, *Les Confessions*, p. 9.

20. Bède, *Histoire ecclésiastique du peuple anglais*, p. 166.

21. Grégoire de Tours, *Histoire des Francs*, t. II, VI, 27.

22. Paul Diacre, *Histoire de Lombards*, IV, 27, p. 86.

23. Ibid., V, 27, p. 116.

24. *Vita Odilae, MGH, Vitae*, VI, pp. 39–40 and *Vita Vincentiani Avolcensis, MGH, Vitae*, V, p. 116.

25. Chrétien Druthmar, *Expositio in Mattheum*, PL 106, col. 1501.

26. Dhuoda, *Manuel pour mon fils*, text published by P. Riché, Sources chrétiennes, no. 225 (Cerf, 1975), I, 7, p. 116.

27. Drawn from a questionnaire of Saxon origin dating from the eighth century, in the Germanic language, *MGH, Capitularia*, I, p. 222.

28. Jonas d'Orléans, *De institutione laïcali*, I, 8, PL 106, col. 135.

29. Loup de Ferrières, *Correspondances*, ed. and trans. L. Levillain (Paris: Les Belles Lettres, 1964), t. II, pp. 42–43.

30. Grégoire de Tours, *Liber vitae patrum*, II.

31. Saint Augustine, *Sermon* 334, PL 38, col. 1447.

32. Etienne, *Vie de saint Wilfrid d'York*, MGH, SRM, VI, p. 213.

33. *Cartulaire de Saint-Vaast d'Arras au XIIᵉ siècle par Guiman*, ed. Van Drival, (Arras, 1875), pp. 155–156.

34. D. Lett, "De l'errance au deuil. Les enfants morts sans baptême et la naissance du *limbus puerorum* aux XIIᵉ-XIIIᵉ siècles," *Actes du XVIᵉ congrès de Flaran (1994), Le premier âge et la petite enfance* (1997).

35. Ruotger de Trêves, *Capitulaire*, c. 23, *MGH, cap. Ep.* I, p. 69.

36. R. Foreville, *Latran I, II, III et Latran IV, Histoire des conciles œcuméniques*, ed. G. Dumeige, vol. VI (Paris: Ed. de l'Orante, 1965), pp. 357–358.

37. A. Alduc-le-Bagousse, "Comportements à l'égard des nouveau-nés et des petits enfants dans les sociétés de la fin de l'Antiquité et du haut Moyen Age," in *L'enfant, son corps et son histoire, Actes des 7ᵉ Journée anthropologiques de Valbonne*, June 1–3, 1994 (Paris: CNRS, 1997).

38. C. Treffort, *Genèse du cimetière chrétien. Etude sur l'accompagnement du mourant, les funérailles, la commémoration des défunts et les lieux d'inhumation à l'époque carolingienne (Enter Loire et Rhin, milieu VIIIᵉ–début XIᵉ siècle)*, doctoral thesis in medieval history, Lyon, under the direction of P. Guichard, September 27, 1994, typescript.

39. Cl. Lorren, "Le village de Saint-Martin de Trainecourt à Mondeville (Calvados) de l'Antiquité au haut Moyen Age," *La Neustrie. Les pays de la Loire de 650 à 850*, International Historical Colloquy, published by H. Atsma, t. II, p. 457.

40. *Archéologie médiévale* 10 (1980): 388–389.

41. C. Niel, "Les inhumations d'enfants au sein de la cour d'Albane, groupe épiscopal de Rouen (Xᵉ-XIᵉ siècles)," in *L'enfant, son corps et son histoire*.

42. V. Fabre and A. Garnotel, "La place de l'enfant dans l'espace des morts. Apports des fouilles du Lunellois," in *L'enfant, sons corps et son histoire*.

43. Lorren, "Le village de Saint-Martin," p. 459.

44. Fabre and Garnotel, "La place de l'enfant dans l'espace des morts."

45. *Un village au temps de Charlemagne. Moines et paysans de l'abbaye de Saint-Denis du VIIᵉ siècle à l'An Mil*, catalogue of the show at the National Museum of Popular Arts and Traditions, November 29, 1988 to April 30, 1989, Paris, 1988, p. 176.

THREE   *Difficult Living Conditions*

1. Grégoire de Tours, *Histoire des Francs*, t. I, IV, 3 and t. I, V, 14.

2. Paul Diacre, *Histoire de Lombards*, IV, 37.

3. R. Le Jan, *Famille et pouvoir dans le monde franc (VIIᵉ–Xᵉ)* (Paris: PU de la Sorbonne, 1995), p. 345.

4. P. Bonnassie, *La Catalogne du milieu du Xe siècle à la fin du XIe siècle. Croissance et mutation d'une société* (Toulouse, 1975–1976), t. I, p. 270.

5. L. Génicot, "On the Evidence of Growth of Population in the West from the Eleventh to the Thirteenth Century," in *Change in the Medieval Society*, ed. S. Thrupp (London, 1965), pp. 14–29.

6. Grégoire de Tours, *Histoire des Francs*, t. II, IX, 38; t. I, II, 29.

7. Bède, *Histoire ecclésiastique du peuple anglais*, p. 159.

8. Grégoire de Tours, *Histoire des Francs*, t. II, VI, 23.

9. Phillippe de Novare, *Les quatre âges de l'homme*, ed. M. de Fréville (Paris: F. Didot, 1888; Johnson Reprint Corporation, New York, 1968), Title 189, p. 103.

10. Grégoire de Tours, *Histoire des Francs*, t. I, V, 22.

11. Ibid., t. I, V, 35.

12. Clovis refers to their first son, Ingomer, who died immediately after his baptism.

13. Grégoire de Tours, *Histoire des Francs*, t. I, II, 29.

14. Ibid., t. I, V, 34.

15. Ibid., t. II, X, 1.

16. R. Glaber, *Histoires*, published by M. Prou (Paris, 1866), cited by G. Duby, *L'an mil*, coll. Archives (Julliard, 1967), pp. 112–113.

17. Grégoire de Tours, *Histoire des Francs*, t. I, III, 7.

18. Bède, *Histoire ecclésiastique du peuple anglais* , p. 167.

19. Grégoire de Tours, *Histoire des Francs*, t. I, III, 6.

20. Ibid., t. I, III, 18.

21. Abbon de Saint-Germain, *Le siège de Paris par les Normands, poème du IXe siècle*, ed. and trans. H. Waquet (Paris: Les Belles Lettres, 1964), pp. 30–31.

22. Bède, *Histoire ecclésiastique du peuple anglais*, pp. 130–131.

23. Paul Diacre, *Histoire de Lombards*, IV, 37. The words in italics are a quote from Virgil, *Géorgiques*, IV, 83.

24. Cassiodore, *Variorum liber*, 8. 33, ed. Theodor Mommsen (Berlin, 1894) (*PL 69*, cols. 763–765).

25. Jordanes, *Histoire des Goths*, introduction, translation, and notes by O. Devillers (Paris: Les Belles Lettres, coll. La Roue à livres, 1995), pp. 54–55.

26. Cited by Bonnassie, *La Catalogne du milieu du Xe siècle à la fin du XIe siècle*, p. 271.

FOUR   *The Education of Children*

1. Ariès, *L'Enfant et la vie familiale sous l'Ancien Régime.*

2. D. Desclais-Berkvam compiled a list of forty-eight terms relating to education in the Middle Ages: D. Desclais-Berkvam, *Enfance et maternité dans la littérature française des XIIe et XIIIe siècles* (Paris: Champion, 1981), p. 95, note 2.

3. *Règle de saint Benoît*, ch. LIII, in *Règles des moines*, ed. J.-P. Lapierre (Paris: Seuil, 1982).

4. *Commentaire de la Règle de saint Benoît*, ed. Bibliotheca Cassinensis, t. IV, ch. LXIII (1880), p. 12, trans. P. Riché, *Ecoles et enseignements dans le haut Moyen Age*, 2nd ed. (1989), p. 363.

5. Egbert de Liège, *Fecunda Ratis*, ed. Voigt (Halle, 1889), p. 179; trans. Riché, *Ecoles et enseignements*, p. 364.

6. Eadmer, *Vita Anselmi*, 22, ed. R. W. Southern (Oxford, 1962), p. 37.

7. Thomas de Cantimpré, *Bonum universale de apibus*, I, 23, ed. Douai (1627), pp. 93–94, cited and translated in A. Lecoy de la Marche, *Le Rire du prédicateur*, ed. J. Berlioz (Brepols, 1992), pp. 152–153.

8. Cited by M. Rouche, *Histoire générale de l'enseignement et de l'éducation en France*, t. I, *Des origines à la Renaissance* (Paris: Nouvelle Librairie de France, 1981), p. 226.

9. *Vita Desiderii, MGH, SRM* 4, pp. 569–570; see Riché, *Ecole et enseignement.*, pp. 20 and 389.

10. Dhuoda, *Manuel pour mon fils.*

11. Ibid., Prologue, pp. 21–22 and I. 7. 18.

12. Ibid., p. 73.

13. Ibid., p. 141.

14. J. Delumeau (ed.), *La religion de ma mère. Le rôle des femmes dans le transmission de la foi* (Paris: Cerf, 1992).

15. Odon de Cluny, *Vita Geraldi Auriliacensis comitis, PL* 133, col. 645.

16. O. Doppelfeld, "Das fränkische Knabengrab unter dem Chor des Kölner Domes," *Germania* 12 (1964): 156–188.

17. *Anonymi vita Hludowici imperatoris*, c. 4, ed. Rau, t. III, p. 264.

18. Ermold le Noir, *Poème sur Louis le Pieux*, ed. and trans. E. Faral (Paris: Champion, 1932), pp. 183–185.

19. *Lamberti Ardensis historia comitum Ghisnensium*, ed. J. Heller, *MGH*, t. XXIV (1879), ch. 90.

20. Ibid.

21. Bède, *Histoire ecclésiastique du peuple anglais*, p. 168.

22. Paul Diacre, *Histoire de Lombards*, book 6, 26, p. 138.

23. R. Le Jan, "Apprentissage militaire, rites de passage et remises d'armes au haut Moyen Age," *Education, apprentissage, initiation au Moyen Age, Actes du Ier colloque international de Montpellier (Université Paul Valéry) de novembre 1991, Cahiers du CRISIMA no. 1* (Montpellier, 1993), p. 222.

24. Grégoire de Tours, *Histoire des Francs*, t. II, VI, 24.

25. Venance Fortunat, *Carmina*, t. IV, 17, v. 8–9, p. 100.

26. Venance Fortunat, *Poèmes*, book IV, 26 (Paris: Les Belles Lettres, 1994), p. 157.

27. *Admonitio Generalis, MGH, Capit.* I, p. 60.

28. Alcuin, *Operum*, Pars. VIII, *PL* 101, col. 1155.

29. Odon de Tournai, *De restauratione abbatiae s. Martini Tornacensis, PL* 180, 43.

30. Théodulf d'Orléans, *Capitula*, I, ch. XX, ed. P. Brommer, *Capitula episcoporum, MGH* (Hanover, 1984), p. 116.

31. *Gesta sanctorum Villariensium, MGH, SS*, XXV, p. 232.

32. See M. De Jong, "Growing up in a Carolingian Monastery. Magister Hildemar and his oblates," *Journal of Medieval History* (1983): 99–128. Also see the summary on oblation: M. De Jong, *In Samuel's Image. Child Oblation in the Early Medieval West* (Bull, 1996).

33. Bède, *Histoire ecclésiastique du peuple anglais*, V. 24.

34. *MGH. Epistolae III*, 2nd ed. (1957), p. 276.

35. Raban Maur, *De oblatione puerorum, PL* 107, col. 419–440.

36. Udalrich, *Consuetudines cluniacenses*, livre III, cap. IX, *PL* 149, col. 747.

37. Etienne de Bourbon, Paris, BNF, Latin ms. 15970, fol. 285, ed. and trans. in de la Marche, *Le Rire du prédicateur*, no. 27, pp. 38–39.

38. Ch. 24, *PL 88*, col. 1054; text ed. and trans. Riché, *Ecole et enseignment*, p. 351.

FIVE   *The Child within the Family*

1. R. Ring, "Early Medieval Peasant Households in Central Italy," *Journal of Family History* 2 (1979): 2–25.

2. Bonnassie, *La Catalogne du milieu du Xe siècle à la fin du XIe siècle*, t. I, p. 267.

3. R. Fossier, *La Terre et les hommes en Picardie* (Paris: Louvain, 1969), pp. 262–273.

4. See in particular the pioneering article by M. Baulant, "La 'famille en miettes': sur un aspect de la démographie du XVIIe siècle," *Famille et société*, special issue of *Annales ESC* 27, no. 4–5 (July–October, 1972): 959–968.

5. See D. Lett, *Enfances, Eglise et familles dans l'Occident chrétien entre le milieu du XIIe siècle et le début du XIVe siècle (Perceptions, pratiques et rôles narratifs)*, doctoral thesis in history presented at EHESS, under the direction of Ch. Klapisch-Zuber, 1995, typescript, pp. 581–611.

6. Ariès, *L'Enfant et la vie familiale sous l'Ancien Régime.*

7. Cited by Le Roy Ladurie, *Montaillou, village occitan de 1294 à 1324*, p. 311.

8. Jean Renart, *L'Escoufle*, ed. Franklin Sweester (Geneva: Droz, 1974; about 1858–1865).

9. Guibert de Nogent, *Autobiographie*, pp. 39–41.

10. William de Cantorbery, *Miracles de Thomas Becket*, book IV, 32, ed. J. G. Robertson, *Materials for History of Archbishop Thomas Becket*, Rolls Series no. 67, vol. 1 and 2.

11. M. B. Salu, *The Ancrene Riwle, The Corpus Ms: Ancrene Wisse* (London, 1955), pp. 102–103.

12. Guillaume Durand, *Rational ou Manuel des divins offices*, ed. and trans. Ch. Barthélemy, 5 vol. (1848–1854), book I, IV, p. 42.

13. Philippe de Novare, *Les quatre âges de l'homme*, art. 8, p. 6.

14. *De b. Margarita Poenitente tertii ord. s. Francisci vita ex mss. auctore f. Juncta Bevagnate*, AS, February III, pp. 298–357.

15. *De b. Angela de Fulginia vita auctore Arnalde*, AS, January I, pp. 186–234.

16. Guillaume de Saint-Thierry, *Physica corporis et animae*, PL, 180, col. 715.

17. Grégoire de Tours, *Histoire des Francs*, book III, ch. V.

18. *Miracles de saint Wulfstan*, ed. R. R. Darlington, *The vita Wulfstani of William of Malmesbury* (London, 1928), book I, 17.

19. G. Raynaud and A. de Montaiglon, *Recueil général et complet des fabliaux des XIIIe et XIVe siècles* (Paris: Librairies des Bibliophiles, 1872–1890), t. IV, CII, pp. 149–150.

20. *Libro e ricordi de Filippo de Bernardo Manetti*, 1429–1456, Biblioteca Nazionale Centrale, Florence. The French translation is by Ch. Klapisch-Zuber, "L'enfant, la mémoire et la mort" (forthcoming).

21. Giovanni Di Pagolo Morelli, *Ricordi*, ed. Vittore Branca (Florence: Felice Le Monnier, 1956), pp. 455–516.

22. Guibert de Nogent, *Autobiographie*, p. 15.

23. *Gest abbatum Orti sancte Marie*, ed. A. W. Wybrands (Leeuwarden, 1879), pp. 26–27; cited and trans. H. Platelle, "L'enfant et la vie familiale au Moyen Age," *Mélanges de Science Religieuse* 39, no. 2 (Lille) (1982): 84.

24. Gilles de Rome, *Le Livre du gouvernement des princes (De Regimine principium)* ed. S. P. Molenaer (1989), p. 192.

25. Raynaud and de Montaiglon, *Recueil général et complet des fabliaux des XIIIe et XIVe siècles*, t. I, V.

26. For all information concerning the nursery, refer to Alexandre-Bidon and Closson, *L'Enfant à l'ombre des cathédrales.*

27. On this topic, see all the articles in Delumeau (ed.), *La religion de ma mère.*

28. Lett, *Enfances, Eglise, et familles*, pp. 341–343.

29. Benedict de Peterborough, *Miracles de Thomas Becket*, book II, p. 41.

30. Guillaume de Saint-Pathus, *Miracles de Saint Louis*, ed. P. B. Fay (Paris: Champion, 1932), pp. 1, 26–27, and 36.

31. Ibid., p. 51.

32. Text published in A. Longnon, *Paris pendant la domination anglaise (1420–1436)* (Paris, 1878), pp. 130–133.

33. Jean Gerson, *Oeuvres complètes*, introduction, text, and notes by Mgr. Glorieux, vol. VIII, *L'Oeuvre spirituelle et pastorale* (Desclée et Cie, 1971), p. 369.

34. Ms. 468 of the municipal library of Tours, fol. 71, ed. and trans. in de la Marche (J. Berlioz, ed.) *Le Rire du prédicateur*, no. 4, pp. 21–22.

35. Lett, *Enfances, Eglise et familles*, pp. 385–392.

36. Benedict de Peterborough, *Miracles de Thomas Becket*, book IV, p. 63.

37. *Miracles de saint Wulfstan*, book II, p. 11.

38. Guillaume de Saint-Pathus, *Miracles de Saint Louis*, p. 51.

39. D. Lett, "La sorella maggiore 'madre sostitutiva' nei miracoli de san Luigi" in "Fratello e sorella," a cura di Angioline Arru e Sofia Boesch Gajano, *Quaderni Storici* 83, a. 28, no. 2 (August 1993): 341–353.

40. Benedict de Peterborough, *Miracles de Thomas Becket*, book III, p. 51.

41. William de Cantorbéry, *Miracles de Thomas Becket*, book VI, 29.

42. Guillaume de Saint-Pathus, *Miracles of Saint Louis*, p. 52.

43. See J. Le Goff, *Saint Louis* (Paris: Fayard, 1996), pp. 37–40 and 707–708.

44. *Salimbene de Adam; un chroniqueur franciscain*, ed. O. Guyot-Jeannin (Brepols, 1995), pp. 122–123.

45. *Vie de Benvenuto Cellini écrite par lui-même*, trans. and notes by M. Beaufreton (Paris: Julliard, 1965), t. 1, pp. 50–51.

46. We have already seen that the value given to maternal nursing had a very important ideological function as well, see chapter 1 above.

47. Aldebrandin de Sienne, *Le régime du corps*, ed. L. Landouzy and R. Pépin (Paris: Champion, 1911).

48. Gilles de Rome, *Le Livre du gouvernement des princes*, p. 217.

49. Jacques de Voragine, *La Légende dorée*, t. II, p. 112.

50. *Daurel et Beton*, lines 724–730.

Part II: Introduction

1. See D. Alexandre-Bidon, "Les livres d'éducation au XIIIe siècle," *Comprendre le XIIIe*, ed. P. Guichard and D. Alexandre-Bidon (Lyon: PUL, 1995), pp. 147–159.

2. See Alexandre-Bidon and Closson, *L'Enfant à l'ombre des cathédrales*, based on ten years of historical research and on new archaeological studies: also see R. Riché and D. Alexandre-Bidon, *L'Enfance au Moyen Age* (Paris: Bibliothèque nationale de France/Seuil, 1994). In this last work can be found a bibliography of 220 French and foreign titles on medieval childhood and abundant iconographical and textual documentation—the "evidence" of the historian.

3. No census was possible before the modern period: the first baptism registers only date back to the 1450s, and they are rare.

4. Alexandre-Bidon and Closson, *L'Enfant à l'ombre des cathédrales.*

5. Riché and Alexandre-Bidon, *L'Enfance au Moyen Age.*

SIX   *Working within the Family*

1. On the importance of teaching children a trade: P.-A. Sigal, "Raymond Lull et l'éducation des enfants d'après la *Doctrina Pueril*," *Raymond Lull et le pays d'Oc,* Cahiers de Fanjeaux 22 (Toulouse: Privat, 1987), pp. 117–139.

2. Author of chronicles, Jean Froissart (1337 to *ca.*1404) also wrote poems, one of which is an autobiography, *L'Espinette amoureuse,* ed. A. Fourrier (Paris: Klinck-sieck, 1972).

3. D. M. Webb, "Some Miracles for Children," in *The Church and Childhood,* ed. D. Wood (1994), p. 191. B. Hanawalt, *The Ties that Bound Peasant Families in Medieval England* (New York: Oxford, 1996), p. 161.

4. *Fabliaux et contes moraux du Moyen Age* (Paris: Le Livre de Poche, 1987), p. 35.

5. J. Favier, *De l'or et des épices, Naissance de l'homme d'affaires au Moyen Age,* (Paris: Fayard, 1987), p. 255.

6. P. Mane, *Calendriers et techniques agricoles (France-Italie/XIIᵉ–XIIIᵉ siècles)* (Paris: Le Sycomore, 1983), p. 136.

7. R. Virgoe, *Les Paston. Une famille anglaise au XVᵉ siècle. Correspondance et vie quotidienne illustrées* (Paris: Hachette, 1990).

8. *L'Enfant au Moyen Age, Senefiance,* no. 9 (Aix-en-Provence, 1980), p. 71, note 33.

9. G. Caster, *Le Commerce de pastel et du l'épicerie à Toulouse, 1450–1561,* (Toulouse: Privat, 1962), p. 43.

10. *Aucassin et Nicolette et autres contes du Jongleur,* ed. A. Pauphilet (Paris: Piazza, 1932), p. 137.

11. *Florilège du Moyen Age* (Paris: Hachette, 1949), p. 61.

12. *Courtois d'Arras, l'enfant prodigue,* ed. J. Dufournet (Paris: GF-Flammarion, 1995), p. 37.

13. *Histoire des jeunes en Occident,* t. I, ed. J.-Cl. Schmitt and G. Lévi (Paris: Seuil, 1996).

14. Pierre de Crescens, *Livre des Profits champestres,* XIIIᶜ siècle, Réserve des livres rares et précieux M 19 (Paris: BNF, Imprints), p. 30.

15. Le Roy Ladurie, *Montaillou, village occitan de 1294 à 1324,* 1982 ed., p. 318.

16. *Le Bon berger, ou le vray régime et gouvernement des bergers et bergères,* ed. P. Lacroix after the 1541 Paris edition (Paris: Liseux, 1879).

17. See Ph. Braunstein, *Un Banquier mis à nu. Autobiographie de Matthäus Schwarz* (Paris: Gallimard, 1992).

18. Le Roy Ladurie, *Montaillou, village occitan de 1294 à 1324,* p. 198.

19. Cl. Gauvard, *"De Grace especial." Crime, Etat et société en France, à la fin du Moyen Age* (Paris, Publ. de la Sorbonne, 1991), p. 336.

20. Text published in *L'Histoire,* no. 180 (September 1994): 37.

21. Le Roy Ladurie, *Montaillou, village occitan de 1294 à 1324,* p. 382.

22. R. Pernoud, *Jeanne d'Arc, par elle-même et par ses témoins* (Paris: Seuil, 1962), pp. 14–16.

23. *L'Artisan dans le péninsule ibérique, RAZO,* no. 14 (Nice: University of Nice, 1993), p. 110.

24. Pernoud, *Jeanne d'Arc*, p. 14.

25. *Péchés et Vertus. Berthold de Ratisbonne*, ed. C. Lecouteux (Paris, 1991), p. 115.

26. J. Dauphiné, "Bonvoisin Da La Riva: *De Quinquaginta curialitatibus ad mensam*," in *Manger et boire au Moyen Age* (Paris: Les Belles Lettres, 1984), pp. 7–20.

27. *Histoire de la France urbaine*, ed. G. Duby (Paris: Seuil, 1980), t. II, "La ville médiévale," pp. 190–191.

28. P. Charbonnier, "L'entrée dans la vie au XVe siècle d'après les lettres de rémission," in *Les Entrées dans la vie. Initiations et aprentissages*, 12th meeting of the Society of Medieval Historians of Higher Public Education (Nancy, 1981) (Nancy: Presses Universitaires de Nancy, 1982), p. 85.

29. Cited in I. Origo, *Le Marchand de Prato, La vie d'un banquier toscan au XIVe siècle* (Paris: Albin Michel, 1989), p. 184.

30. F. Franceschi, "Les enfants au travail dans l'industrie textile florentine des XIVe et XVe siècles," *Les Dépendances au travail, Médiévales*, no. 30 (1996): 69–82.

31. Favier, *De l'or et des épices*, p. 76.

32. J. Heers, *Gênes au XVe siècle* (Paris: SEVPEN, 1961), p. 313.

SEVEN *Apprenticeships*

1. F. Michaud-Fréjaville, "Bons et loyaux services. Les contrats d'apprentissage en Orléannais (1380–1480)," in *Les Entrées dans la vie*, p. 202.

2. *L'Artisan*, p. 106.

3. J. Verdon, *Les Françaises pendant la guerre de Cent ans* (Paris: Perrin, 1991), p. 179.

4. C. Béghin, "Entre ombre et lumière, quelque aspects du travail des femmes à Montpellier (1293–1308)," in *Les Dépendances*.

5. Michaud-Fréjaville, "Bons et loyaux services," p. 186.

6. Béghin, "Entre ombre et lumièr," p. 50, note 28.

7. Michaud-Fréjaville, "Bons et loyaux services," p. 205, note 59.

8. The text appears in *Chaucer's World*, ed. E. Rickert (New York and London: Columbia University Press, 1962).

9. Franceschi, "Les enfants au travail dans l'industrie textile florentine."

10. Reproduction in *Le Printemps des génies. Les enfants prodiges*, ed. M. Sacquin (Paris: BNF/Laffont, 1993), p. 28.

11. R. Vaultier, *Le Folklore en France durant le guerre de Cent Ans d'après les lettres de rémission* (Paris: Guénégaud, 1965), p. 142.

12. Béghin, "Entre ombre et lumièr," p. 47.

13. The case of a little girl: *Histoire des femmes*, t. II, "Le Moyen Age," ed. Ch. Klapisch-Zuber (Paris: Plon, 1991), p. 417.

14. P. Wolff, *Regards sur le Midi médiéval* (Toulouse: Privat, 1978), p. 415.

15. Michaud-Fréjaville, "Bons et loyaux services," p. 191.

16. Ibid., p. 185.

17. *L'Artisan*, p. 91.

18. P. Bernardi, "Relations familiales et rapports professionnels chez les artisans du bâtiment en Provence à la fin du Moyen Age," in *Les Dépendances au travail*, pp. 55–68.

19. A. Stella, *La Révolte des Ciompi. Les hommes, les lieux, le travail* (Paris: EHESS, 1993), pp. 114–115.

20. Franceschi, "Les enfants au travail dans l'industrie textile florentine," p. 77.

21. Stella, *La Révolte*, p. 117.

22. Franceschi, "Les enfants au travail dans l'industrie textile florentine."

23. Théophile, *Essai sur divers arts*, published by C. de l'Escalopier, reprinted by Laget (Nogent-le-Roi: Editions Librairie des Arts et Métiers, 1977), p. 255.

24. *Livre des Simples Médecines*, Bruxelles, Bibl. Roy Albert Ier, ms IV. 1024, fol. 116, ed. in facsimile by C. Opsomer (Bruxelles).

25. *Vie de Benvenuto Cellini*, p. 52, note 1.

26. F. Avril and N. Raynaud, *Les Manuscrits à peinture en France, 1440–1520* (Paris: BNF/Flammarion, 1993), pp. 80, 326–327.

27. Béghin, "Entre ombre et lumièr," p. 48, note 22.

28. Paris, BNF, Hebrew Ms. 402. See M. Garel, *D'une Main forte. Manuscrits hébreux des collections françaises* (Paris: Seuil/BNF, 1991), p. 166.

29. Stella, *La Révolte*, p. 120.

30. Text cited in Riché, *Ecole et enseignment*, p. 226.

31. Franceschi, "Les enfants au travail dans l'industrie textile florentine," pp. 71–73.

32. *L'Artisan*, p. 106.

33. *Vie de Benvenuto Cellini*, p. 59.

34. Franceschi, "Les enfants au travail dans l'industrie textile florentine," p. 79.

35. Bernardi, "Relations familiales et rapports professionnels," p. 65.

36. Franceschi, "Les enfants au travail dans l'industrie textile florentine," p. 81.

37. L. Stouff, *Arles à la fin du Moyen Age* (Lille: Université de Provence-Lille, 1986), p. 298.

38. J. Rossiaud, *La Prostitution au Moyen Age* (Paris: Flammarion, 1988), p. 41.

39. Cases cited by Verdon, *Les Françaises*, p. 180.

40. Gauvard, *"De Grace especial." Crime, Etat et société en France*, p. 418.

41. Le Roy Ladurie, *Montaillou, village occitan de 1294 à 1324*, p. 382.

42. Franceschi, "Les enfants au travail dans l'industrie textile florentine," p. 81.

43. Quoted in E. Garin, *L'Education de l'homme moderne. La pédagogie de la Renaissance* (Paris, 1968), p. 26.

44. *Vie de Benvenuto Cellini*, p. 59.

45. On this subject, see J. Heers, *Le Clan familial au Moyen Age* (Paris: PUF, 1974).

46. Heers, *Gênes au XVe siècle*, p. 555.

47. Ibid., pp. 370, 402, 554.

48. H. Bresc, "Documents siciliens," in *Le Corps souffrant, maladies et médications, RAZO*, Cahiers du centre d'études médiévales de Nice, no. 4 (Nice) (1984): 113–114.

49. Origo, *Le Marchand de Prato*, p. 190.

50. Ibid., p. 196.

51. Ibid., p. 193.

52. Heers, *Gênes au XVe siècle*, p. 554.

53. National Archives, A 1160 (AE II 2984).

EIGHT   *Children on the Streets*

1. For Italy: *Salimbene de Adam*, p. 262. For England, letter from the archbishop Robert Brayeroke, *Chaucer's World*, p. 48.

2. E. Crouzet-Pavan, "Une fleur du mal?" in *Histoire des jeunes*, pp. 242–243.

3. Ch. Klapisch-Zuber, "L'Enfant, la mémoire et la mort," forthcoming.

4. H. Martin, *Le Métier de prédicateur à la fin du Moyen Age, 1350–1520* (Paris: Cerf, 1988), p. 57.

5. *Journal d'un bourgeois de Paris de 1405 à 1449*, ed. C. Beaune (Paris: Hachette, 1990), p. 70.

6. Jean Froissart, *L'Espinette amoureuse*, ed. A. Fourrier (Paris: Klinck-sieck, 1972), text published in M. Gally and C. Marchello-Nizia, *Littératures de l'Europe médiévale* (Paris: Magnard, 1985), p. 439.

7. Pernoud, *Jeanne d'Arc*, pp. 17–19.

8. Cited by Ph. Contamine, *La vie quotidienne pendant la guerre de Cent Ans, France et Angleterre* (Paris: Hachette, 1976), p. 160.

9. *Chaucer's World.*

10. Text published in *Chaucer's World*, p. 100.

11. A. D. Côte d'Or, B 3807, p. 23.

12. Gauvard, *"De Grace especial." Crime, Etat et société en France*, p. 279.

13. *Péchés et vertus*, pp. 115–116.

14. Saint Augustine, *Confessions*, Book 2, chs. 4–9.

15. Gauvard, *"De Grace especial." Crime, Etat et société en France*, p. 355.

16. J. Dufournet, ed., *Le Garçon et l'aveugle* (Paris: Champion, 1982).

17. Ibid., p. 66.

18. *Journal d'un bourgeois*, pp. 399 and 442.

19. Klapisch-Zuber, "L'Enfant, la mémoire et la mort."

20. Gauvard, *"De Grace especial." Crime, Etat et société en France*, p. 279.

21. See Rossiaud, *La Prostitution au Moyen Age*, p. 41.

22. *Péchés et vertus*, p. 116.

23. Rossiaud, *La Prostitution au Moyen Age*, pp. 115–116.

24. Ibid., p. 46.

25. Franceschi, "Les enfants au travail dans l'industrie textile florentine," p. 78.

26. See P.-A. Sigal, "Comment l'Eglise a sauvé les enfants abandonnés," *L'Histoire*, no. 161 (December 1992): 18–24, and *Enfance abandonnée et société en Europe, XVᵉ–XXᵉ siècle* (Rome: Ecole française de Rome, 1991).

27. *Journal d'un bourgeois*, p. 164.

28. B. Geremek, *Les Marginaux parisiens aux XIVᵉ et XVᵉ siècles* (Paris, 1976), pp. 276 and 392.

29. K. Simon-Muscheid, "Indispensable et caché. Le travail quotidien des enfants au bas Moyen Age et à la Renaissance," in *Les Dépendances au travail*, p. 100.

NINE **The Child in the Castle**

1. *Le Château médiéval, forteresse habitée*, ed. J.-M. Poisson (Paris: DAF, 1990), p. 19.

2. G. Arnaud d'Agnel, *Les Comptes du roi René* (Paris: Picard et fils, 1910), t. 111, no. 3511.

3. *La Chronique*, ed. C. Bruneau, t. IV, 1500–1525 (Metz: Sociéte d'histoire et d'archéologie de la Lorraine, 1933).

4. Gaston Phébus, *Le Livre de la chasse*, ed. R. and A. Bossuat, facsimile (Paris: Philippe Lebaud, 1986), p. 90.

5. Ibid.

6. Heldris de Cornouailles, ed. L. Thorpe (Cambridge, 1972), text quoted in *Littératures de l'Europe médiévale*, p. 272.

7. Hanawalt, *The Ties That Bound*, p. 185.

8. Crouzet-Pavan, "Une fleur du mal?"

9. Ed. by L. Lecestre, 2 vol. (Paris: SATF, 1887–1889).

10. Arch. nat., JJ 185/247.

11. G. Duby, *Guillaume le Maréchal ou le meilleur chevalier du monde* (Paris: Fayard, 1984), pp. 80–81.

12. F. Lehoux, *Jean de France, duc de Berry. Sa vie, son action politique,* t. III (Paris: Picard, 1968).

13. Ibid., pp. 29–33.

14. Christine de Pizan, *Le Livre des trois vertus*, critical edition, introduction and notes by Charity Cannon Willard (Paris: Champion, 1989), p. 59, ch. "Ci devise du tiers enseignement de Prudence, qui est comment la sage princesse sera soigneuse de se prendre garde sur l'estat et gouvernement de ses enfants."

15. *The Book of Babees*, text quoted in *Chaucer's World*, trans. G. Alexandre.

16. E. Roy, "Un régime de santé pour les petits enfants at l'hygiène de Gargantua," in *Mélanges Picot* (Paris, 1913). See the commentary in Alexandre-Bidon and Closson, *L'Enfant à l'ombre des cathédrales*, p. 140.

17. Aelred Squire, O.P., *Aelred of Rievaulx: A Study* (London: SPCK, 1969), p. 13.

18. *Histoire des femmes,* t. 2, p. 110.

19. Jean Renart, *Guillaume de Dôle ou le roman de la rose*, ed. F. Lecoy (Paris: Champion, 1962), text cited in *Littératures de l'Europe médiévale*, p. 295.

20. *Le Livre des trois vertus*, p. 106.

21. Ed. A. de Montaiglon (Paris, 1854).

22. G. Duby, "Au XIIe siècle: the "jeunes" in la société aristocratique," *Annales ESC* 2 (1964): see p. 839.

23. 7th Partida, 1260, put into effect 1340. See A. Ruiz Moreno, *La Medicina en la legislacion medioeval espanola* (Buenos Aires: El Ateneo, 1946), p. 147. My thanks to Pr. J. Shatzmiller who pointed this astonishing text out to me.

24. *The Book of Babees*, in *Chaucer's World*.

25. Eihlard von Oberg, *Tristant*. On Tristan's childhood, see J. Bédier, *Le roman de Tristan et Iseult* (Paris: Piazza, 1946), p. 4.

26. A. D. Meuse, B 503.

27. *Vie de Benvenuto Cellini*, p. 52.

28. *Péchés et Vertus*, p. 114.

29. Guibert de Nogent, *Autobiographie*, I, p. 5.

30. *Le Livre des trois vertus*, p. 60.

31. D. Alexandre-Bidon, "Livres d'enfance et de jeunesse au Moyen Age," *Histoire du livre de jeunesse. De Charlemagne à Guizot,* t. I (Paris: Picard, forthcoming).

TEN   *The Child at School*

1. J. Le Goff, *Marchands et banquiers du Moyen Age* (Paris: PUF, 1956), p. 100.

2. S. Guilbert, "Les écoles rurales en Champagne au XVe siècle. Enseignement et promotion sociale," *Les Entrées dans le vie*, pp. 127–147, see p. 138.

3. Ibid., p. 207.

4. L. Carolus-Barré, "Les écoles capitulaires et les collèges de Soissons au Moyen Age et au XVIᵉ siècle," *Enseignement et vie intellectuelle (IXᵉ–XVIᵉ siècle)*, Actes du 95th congrès national des Sociétés Savantes, Reims, 1970 (Paris: Bibliothèque nationale de France, 1975), see p. 168.

5. Riché, *Ecoles*, p. 193.

6. Guilbert, "Les écoles rurales," p. 130.

7. R. Fédou,"Le Moyen Age: de Leidrade à Gerson," *Education et pédagogie à Lyon de l'Antiquité à nos jours*, ed. A. Vanzini (Lyon: Centre lyonnaise d'études et de recherches en sciences de l'éducation, 1993), pp. 19–37, see p. 32.

8. Paris, BNF, Latin ms. 9473.

9. Fédou, "Le Moyen Age: de Leidrade à Gerson."

10. P. Desportes, "L'Enseignement à Reims aux XIIIᵉ et XIVᵉ siècles," *Enseignement et vie intellectuelle*, I, pp. 97–122, see p. 109.

11. Fédou,"Le Moyen Age: de Leidrade à Gerson," p. 30.

12. Carolus-Barré, "Les écoles capitulaires et les collèges," pp. 195 and 202.

13. Ibid., p. 146.

14. Guilbert, "Les écoles rurales," pp. 131–132, also pp. 128 and 142.

15. Text of the statutes published in *Sources d'histoire médiévale, IXᵉ–milieu du XIVᵉ siècle*, ed. G. Brunel and E. Lalou (Paris: Larousse, 1992), pp. 604–606.

16. P. Desportes, *Reims et les Rémois aux XIIIᵉ et XIVᵉ siècles* (Paris: Picard, 1979), p. 206.

17. M. Mollat, *Le Commerce maritime normand à la fin du Moyen Age. Etude d'histoire économique et sociale* (Paris: Plon, 1952), p. 533.

18. *L'Allemagne au XIIIᵉ siècle*, ed. M. Parisse (Paris: Picard, 1994), pp. 210–211.

19. *Histoire des femmes*, t. II, p. 311.

20. Ch. Klapisch-Zuber, "L'Enfant, la mémoire et la mort."

21. Guilbert, "Les écoles rurales."

22. Fédou, "Le Moyen Age: de Leidrade à Gerson," p. 32.

23. G. Sivéry, *Terroirs et communautés rurales dans l'Europe occidentale au Moyen Age* (Lille: Presses universitaires de Lille, 1990), p. 212.

24. Guilbert, "Les écoles rurales," pp. 128 and 142.

25. H. Martin, "L'Eglise éducatrice. Messages apparents, contenus sous-jacents," in *Educations médiévales*, p. 98.

26. B. Chevalier, *Tours, ville royale (1356–1520). Origine et développement d'une capitale à la fin du Moyen Age* (Louvain: Vander/Nauwelaert; Chambray-les-Tours: CLD, 1983), p. 557.

27. Desportes, *Reims et les Rémois.*"

28. "Conte de la prieure," ed. J.-P. Foucher (Paris: Le Livre de Poche, 1974), p. 207.

29. *Op. cit.*, p. 178.

30. Guilbert, "Les écoles rurales," p. 134.

31. Michaud-Fréjaville, "Bons et loyaux services," p. 205, note 59.

32. Verger, *Educations médiévales*, p. 7.

33. Ph. Contamine, "Livre et société dans la France de la fin du Moyen Age," in *Les Manuscrits à peinture en France, 1440–1520*, preface by F. Avril and N. Raynaud (Paris: BNF, Flammarion, 1993), pp. 8–10, see p. 9.

34. H.-J. Martin, *Histoire et pouvoirs de l'écrit* (Paris: Perrin, 1994), p. 310.

35. Contamine, "Livre et société."

36. Sivéry, *Terroirs*, pp. 210–212.

37. Chevalier, *Tours, ville royale*, p. 207.

38. F. Gasparri, "Note sur l'enseignement de l'écriture aux XVe–XVIe siècles," *Scrittura e civiltà* 2 (1978) and "Ensignement et technique de l'écriture de Moyen Age à la fin du XIIIe siècle," *Scrittura e civiltà* 7 (1983): 201–222, see p. 209.

39. *Le Livre du Vaillant des habitants de Lyon en 1388*, ed. E. Philippon (Lyon: Audin, 1927), pp. 50–53.

40. H. Amouric and D. Foy, "Liberté? Contraintes et privilèges. Les artisanats de la terre et du verre dans la Provence médiévale," *Les Libertés au Moyen Age*, Actes du colloque de Montbrison (Montbrison, 1987), pp. 252–280, see p. 262.

41. Municipal archives of Lyon, BB 63. Quoted in F. Godefroy, *Dictionnaire de l'ancienne langue francaise et de tous ses dialectes du IXe au XVe siècle*, 10 vol. (Paris: new ed. 1937 [re-ed. Geneva-Paris: Slatkine, 1982]), t. VI, p. 335.

42. *Sources d'Histoire médiévale*, pp. 603–604.

43. Ibid., p. 602.

44. Paris, BNF, ms NAF 1465, quoted in the works of F. Gasparri (see above note 38).

45. Carolus-Barré, "Les écoles capitulaires et les collèges," p. 148.

46. L. Stouff, *La table provençale. Boire et manger en Provence à la fin du Moyen Age*, ed. Barthélémy (1996), pp. 177–180.

47. Vaultier, *Le Folklore*, p. 183.

48. Aubrun, *La Vie de saint Etienne de Aubazine* (1970), p. 69.

49. Text printed in *Formes médiévales du conte merveilleux*, ed. J. Berlioz, C. Brémond, and C. Velay-Valentin (Paris: Stock, 1989), pp. 133–134.

50. Desportes, "L'Enseignement," p. 108, note 6.

51. P. Champion, "Pièces joyeuses du XVe siècle," *Revue de philologie française* 21 (1907): 161–196.

52. *Devinettes françaises du Moyen Age*, ed. B. Roy (Paris, Vrin; Montreal: Bellarmin, 1977), p. 138, no. 394.

53. Lydgate, "The Testament," *Minor Poems*, pp. 352–353. Text published in *Chaucer's World*, p. 98.

54. Froissart, *L'Espinette amoureuse; Littératures de l'Europe médiévale*, p. 438.

55. Ibid.

56. Klapisch-Zuber, "L'Enfant, la mémoire et la mort."

57. Desportes, "L'Enseignement" p. 109.

58. Y. Dossat, "Université et Inquisition à Toulouse: la fondation du collège Saint-Raymond (1250)," in *Enseignement et vie intellectuelle*, t, I, pp. 227–238.

59. Aldebrandin de Sienne, *Le Régime du corps*, ed. L. Landouzy and R. Pépin (Paris: 1911), text published in *Littératures de l'Europe médiévale*, p. 210.

60. Duby, "Au XIIe siècle: les jeunes," see p. 837.

61. D. Foy, *Le Verre médiéval et son artisanat* (Paris: CNRS, 1989), pp. 60 and 87.

62. *Courtois d'Arras*.

63. Case mentioned in S. Roux, *La Rive gauche des escholiers* (Paris: Ed. Christian, 1992), p. 73.

64. Avril and Raynaud, *Les Manuscrits*, p. 20.

65. Le Goff, *Marchand et banquiers*, p. 106.

66. Ed. J. Misrahi and C.A. Knudson (Droz: T. L. F., 1965).

67. Le Goff, *Marchands and banquiers*, p. 83.

GLOSSARY

Words included in the glossary are marked with an asterisk the first time they appear in the text.

Catechumen: (from the Greek *katēkhoumenos*) a novice whom one instructs in order to allow him to receive baptism.

Churching: a blessing given to a woman after giving birth which permits her to be reintegrated into the Church. During the forty days immediately following birth, the young mother must not, in theory, leave her room and must limit her contact with others as much as possible, her labor, a consequence of the sin of the flesh, having tainted her for a time.

Compline: the last liturgical office of the day, which is recited just after vespers or after the last evening meal, before going to bed (about six or seven o'clock).

Compute: (from the Latin *computare*) a way of calculating the degrees of relationship. In particular, we distinguish the Roman (or civil) system of computation, which counts as many degrees as there are positions of relationship on the genealogical tree relating an individual to another by their common ancestor, and the Germanic (or ecclesiastical) system of computation which calculates the degree according to the number of generations separating two individuals from their common ancestor.

Exemplum (plural: *exempla*): a brief and edifying narrative which medieval preachers inserted in their sermons to convince the audience of a beneficial lesson.

Fosterage (from the verb "to foster"): an aristocratic practice which consisted of entrusting a young noble to another lord for his education.

Hagiography: (from the Greek *agios*, saint and *graphein*, to write) the science and all the sources relating to the lives (*vitae*) and miracles (*miracula*) of the saints. A *hagiographer* is a cleric who writes narratives of this kind.

Homéliares: (from the Greek, *homilia*, meeting of men) collections of sermons, homilies, or commentaries on the Scripture, regrouped according to the cycle of annual holidays and read before the liturgical service.

Hours (book of): a book used by the laity containing the prayers to say at different "hours" of the day (matins, vespers, complines, etc.) and organized by "offices" or "masses" (of Our Lady, of the dead, etc.).

Illuminations: painted images in the book manuscripts on parchment or paper. From *illuminare*, to light up.

Infans: a term which, in the Latin texts of the Middle Ages, usually designates a very small child (less than two or three years old). Literally the *infans* is "the one who cannot speak": *qui fari non potest.*

Lauds: a morning liturgical office composed principally of psalms, which is celebrated, in summer, immediately after matins.

Manse: in the property system of the early Middle Ages, the manse was the unit of use which included the dwelling place, its inhabitants, and an area of land which normally had to suffice to feed one family.

Matins: the first liturgical office of the morning, between one and three o'clock (according to the season and the region) in which one sings and recites the breviary.

Mi-parties: (French, for half, or two, parts) the name given to the livery in two opposing colors worn by the servants or pages of a lord.

Pedobaptism: baptism of little children.

Polyptychs: this is a matter of private documents on property management from the Carolingian period. The name comes from the external appearance of the document which was folded many times. They showed a series of assessments of revenues that the landowner collected from his lands and the peasants who worked them.

Reconquista: the reconquest by Christians of Arab territories in Spain, between the eighth and fifteenth centuries.

Simples: medicinal herbs. Beginning from Carolingian times, herbarium manuscripts assembled information about these plants used in medicine as well as in cooking.

Wergeld: (Germanic term derived from *wer* or *vir*, which means "man," and *geld*, which means "money;" literally, "the price of the man") in the early Middle Ages, it was a matter of a compensatory fine paid to the victim or his family in the case of an injury or death.

SELECTED BIBLIOGRAPHY

Alexandre-Bidon, D., and M. Closson. *L'enfant à l'ombre des cathédrales.* Lyon: Presses Universitaires de Lyon, 1985.

Ariès, Ph., *L'enfant et la vie familiale sous l'Ancien Régime.* Paris: Plon, 1960: new ed. Seuil, 1973.

Arnold, K. *Kind und Gesellschaft in Mitteralter und Renaissance.* Paderborn: Verlag F. Schnöningh, 1980.

Bambini santi, rappresentazioni dell'infanzia e modelli agiografici. Ed. Anna Benvenuti Papi and Elena Giannarelli. Torino: Rosenberg and Sellier, 1991.

Bologne, J.-Cl. *La naissance interdite. Stérilité, avortement, contraception au Moyen Age.* Paris: Olivier Orban, 1988.

Boswell, J. *The Kindness of Strangers. The Abandonment of Children in Western Europe from late Antiquity to the Renaissance.* New York: Pantheon Books, 1988. French edition: *Au bon cœur des inconnus, Les enfants abandonnés de l'Antiquité à la Renaissance.* Paris: Gallimard, 1993.

The Church and Childhood. Ed. D. Wood. *Studies in Church History* 31. Oxford, 1994.

Desclais-Berkvam, D. *Enfance et maternité dans la littérature française des XIIe et XIIIe siècles.* Paris: Champion, 1981.

Education, Apprentissages, Initiation au Moyen Age. Actes du 1er colloque international de Montpellier (Université Paul Valéry) November 1991. *Cahiers du CRISIMA* no. 1. Montpellier, November 1993.

Enfance abandonée et société en Europe, XIVe-XXe siècle. Actes du colloque de Rome, January 1987; Ecole française de Rome, January 30-31, 1987. 1991.

Enfant et société, Annales de Démographie Historique. Paris: Mouton, 1973.

L'Enfant Recueil de la société Jean Bodin. t. 36, vols. 2 and 5. Brussels, 1976.

L'Enfant au Moyen Age. Sénéfiance no. 9. Aix-en-Provence: CUERMA, 1980.

Les Entrées dans la vie, initiations et apprentissages. Actes du XIIe congrès de la Société des historiens médiévistes de l'enseignement supérieur public, Nancy, 1981. Nancy, 1982.

Famille et parenté dans l'Occident médiéval. Ed. J. Le Goff and G. Duby. Actes du colloque de Paris, June 1974. Rome: Ecole française, 1977.

Flandrin, J.-L. *L'Eglise et le contrôle des naissances.* Paris, 1970.

Flandrin, J.-L. *Familles, parentés, maison, sexualité dans l'ancienne société.* Paris, 1976.

Giallongo, A. *Il bambino medievale. Educazione ed infanzia nel Medioevo.* Bari: Dedalo, 1990.

Goodich, M. *From Birth to Old Age. The Human Life Cycle in Medieval Thought, 1250–1350.* New York and London: University of Haïfa, 1989.

Goody, J. *L'évolution de la famille et du mariage en Europe.* Paris: Armand Colin, 1985.

Hanawalt, B. A. Ed. "The Evolution of Adolescence in Europe." *Journal of Family History* 17, no. 4, 1992.

Hanawalt, B. A., *Growing Up in Medieval London, the Experience of Childhood in History.* New York: Oxford University Press, 1993.

Herlihy, D., and C. Klapisch-Zuber. *Les Toscans et leurs familles. Une étude de* catasto *florentin de 1427.* Paris: Presses de la Fondation nationale des sciences politiques, 1978.

Histoire de la famille. Ed. A, Burguiere,. C. Klapisch-Zuber, M. Segalen, and F. Zonabend. t. I. Paris: Armand Colin, 1986.

Klapisch-Zuber, C. *La maison et le nom. Stratégies et rituels dans l'Italie de la Renaissance.* Paris: l'EHESS, 1990.

Laurent, S. *Naître au Moyen Age. De la conception à la naissance. La grossesse et l'accouchement (XIIᵉ–XVᵉ siècles).* Paris: Le Léopard d'Or, 1989.

Liens de famille, Vivre et choisir sa parenté. Médiévales no. 19. Ed. Ch. Klapisch-Zuber. Saint-Denis: Presses universitaires de Vincennes, fall 1990.

de Mause, L. Ed. *The History of Childhood.* New York: Harper and Row, 1974.

Metz, R. *La femme et l'enfant dans le droit canonique médiéval.* Reprint. London: Variorum, 1985.

Niccoli, O. Ed. *Infanzie: funzioni di un gruppo liminale dal mondo classico all'Età moderna.* Florence: Ponte alle Grazie, 1993.

Les Relations de parenté dans le monde médiéval enfiance. Senefiance no. 26. pub. of Aix-en-Provence: CUERMA, 1986.

Riché, P. *Ecoles et enseignements dans le haut Moyen Age.* 2nd ed. Paris: Picard, 1989.

Riché, P. *Education et culture dans l'Occident barbare, VIᵉ–VIIIᵉ siècles.* Paris: L'Univers historique, Seuil, 1962; reprint Point Seuil, 1995.

Riché, P., and D. Alexandre-Bidon. *L'enfance au Moyen Age.* Paris: Seuil, Bibliothèque nationale de France, 1994.

Schmitt, J.-Cl., and G. Levi. *Histoire des jeunes en Occident.* Paris: Seuil, 1996.

Schultz, J. A. *The Knowledge of Childhood in the German Middle Ages, 1100–1350.* Philadelphia: University of Pennsylvania Press, 1995.

Shahar, S. *Childhood in the Middle Ages.* London and New York: Routledge, 1990.

INDEX

Danièle Alexandre–Bidon is Fellow at the University Lumière–Lyon II and co-author of *A réveiller les morts: La mort au quotidien dans l'Occident médiéval.*

Didier Lett is Assistant Professor in Medieval History at the University Versailles Saint-Quentin-en-Yvelines and author of *Enfances et familles sous le regard de l'Eglise XIIe–XIVe centuries.*